Texas
Outdoor
Adventure
Guide for Kids

Texas Outdoor
Adventure
Guide for Kids

by
Melissa Maupin

E PRESS

For my father, Harold Shearer, who shared with me
his appreciation of the natural world,
and for my mother, Ivy Shearer,
who taught me to love
the written word

Publisher and Editor: Georg Zappler
Designer: Barbara M. Whitehead
Printing Coordnator: Muke Diver

ISBN: 1-885696-28-0

Contents

Introduction

As a child, I recall family car trips across Texas, heading off for a vacation or moving to a new city to live. Scrunched in the back seat between my brother and sister, my thoughts were often occupied with trying to get comfortable or with whether I could wait until the next restroom stop.

My father, though, was usually preoccupied with looking out the window, and often he discussed with us what he saw. As one landscape blended into another, he would point out trees and flowers, a bird circling in the air and another perched on a fence-post. He talked about the lay of the land, how it had formed, and how people and animals existed there in the past. At times he would spot a deer and pull over so we could all get a look. Even though I would strain to focus where his finger pointed, I often saw only a frustrating jumble of tree limbs and grass.

Back then, if I had my choice during these trips, I probably would've passed the time listening to the radio, reading comic books, or giggling with my siblings. It wasn't until later in life that I appreciated the fact that my father had instilled in me a love and respect for Texas, for the expanse of the land, and for the plants and animals that live here. Now that I have children of my own, I too want them to learn respect for nature and to cherish time spent in the beauty of Texas outdoors. That is the goal of this book—to give children and their parents, teachers, and youth leaders a guide to exploring and appreciating the majesty and diversity of nature in Texas.

Each chapter of the book lists and describes a different area of nature exploration, from quiet study in a city setting to participation in challenging, active eco-sports. When appropriate, each listing in this book is followed by initials in brackets identifying the area where the program or place is located in the state. These areas represent the seven major topographical regions of Texas and coincide with those described in brochures and other information available from the Texas Parks & Wildlife Department.

I hope this guide will assist adults in exploring the natural world with children so that another generation of kids can grow up learning to appreciate and respect the great Texas outdoors.

Geographic Locations and their Abbreviations
used in this Book:

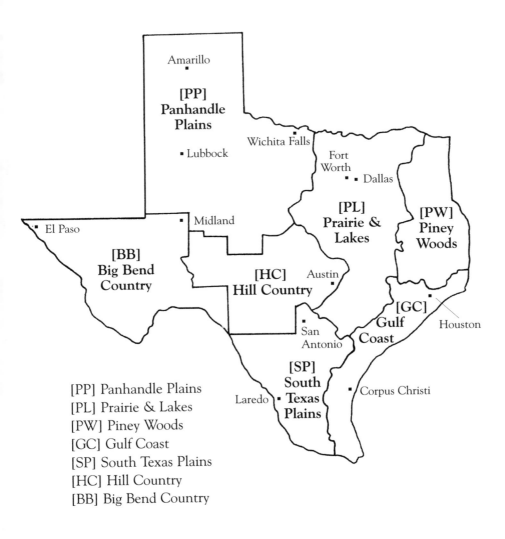

[PP] Panhandle Plains
[PL] Prairie & Lakes
[PW] Piney Woods
[GC] Gulf Coast
[SP] South Texas Plains
[HC] Hill Country
[BB] Big Bend Country

Chapter One

❧

Kids & Texas Outdoors

Texas is spread out far and wide, with plenty of room for kids to roam. Those new to Texas may also be surprised at the state's wide diversity of terrain and plant and animal life. Every section has a distinctive look and offers children unique opportunities to get outside and experience nature first hand. In west Texas, kids can hike up a mountain trail; or they may prefer a quiet lake in the panhandle plains to wet their hook. They can stroll along the beach and watch the sun come up over the vast waters of the Gulf of Mexico or watch it set in brilliant colors over prickly pear in the Chihuahuan Desert. Children can climb a craggy rock in the hill country, off-road bike through a piney wood forest in east Texas, or hunt for deer in the south Texas brush country. No matter what type of land one loves and how one chooses to explore it, there is something for everyone in Texas.

State Parks and Wildlife Management Areas

When Texas entered the Union in 1845, it voted to keep its land out of federal control. But over the following years, it doled out tracts of land to encourage settlers to populate the state. Those lands that were not granted to settlers were eventually sold to finance public works.

As a result, Texas occupies 267,000 square miles, yet only about 2% of the land is publicly owned. This is both a blessing and a curse. Privately held lands are often maintained better by landowners than are those open to the public, and some remain in a natural state with little or no development. The downside is that these lands are closed to the general public's use.

In order to ensure an adequate supply of public land for parks and recreation, the state of Texas now has to buy it back or receive parcels of land in the form of grants. Lately, the Texas Parks & Wildlife Department has been acquiring land in urban areas such as Houston and Dallas to make natural areas more accessible to a greater number of urban children as well as to other citizens.

The state of Texas is currently guardian to five forests and over one hundred nature and historical parks. The state operates state parks, fish hatcheries, historical parks, natural areas, and wildlife management areas. Many state parks are situated near lakes or coastal waters, and all offer unique opportunities to view, explore, and appreciate the state's natural beauty. State parks vary in the amount of development and facilities available to travelers. Some are very primitive, with only camp sites, while others have meeting rooms, nature centers, scheduled recreational activities, and cabins to rent.

Wildlife management areas are generally more primitive than

parks, with the emphasis on the wildlife rather than on the human visitor. Often they have limited facilities and no camping or picnic areas. Wildlife management areas are dedicated to research and demonstrating to landowners and others effective land use and wildlife management.

Before taking kids on a trip to any state park, call the Texas Parks & Wildlife Department (TPW) or the specific park for a brochure. Since state parks are popular family destinations, always make reservations when you plan to camp in one. Parents and group leaders can reserve camp sites, group facilities, and cabins up to eleven months in advance, and reservations must be made at least three days before the planned date of stay. To make reservations for all parks except the Indian Lodge in Davis Mountain State Park and the Texas State Railroad, call TPW at 512-389-8900, Monday through Friday from 9:00 A.M. to 6:00 P.M. To cancel reservations, call 512-389-8910. The Indian Lodge number is 915-426-3254, and the Texas State Railroad number is 1-800-442-8951.

State Park Fees

Entrance fees for state parks vary with each park, but are on a per-person basis. The majority of parks currently charge $2 per person or less, but this is subject to change, so call in advance. The good news is that children 12 and under get in free to all state parks. Nonprofit youth groups may also purchase an annual $100 Youth Group Permit which will grant the group and its adult supervisors unlimited park entry for up to 50 people. Youth members must be 18 years old or younger.

Families who frequently visit state parks may want to purchase a Texas Conservation Passport. The Silver Passport costs $25 annually and allows the individual and those traveling with him or her to enter wildlife management areas at certain times, as well as special discounts. The Gold Passport is a windshield decal that costs $50 annually and grants unlimited access to the holder and traveling companions to state parks, as well as free tours of state historical parks and access to wildlife management areas at certain times. Families may purchase duplicate decals for other vehicles for $15 each. With either passport you will receive the *Texas Conservation Passport Journal,* a quarterly publication with short articles and a list of upcoming events, tours, and recreational events in state parks and management areas.

For more exciting news about what is happening in state parks every month, check the *Texas Parks & Wildlife* magazine's outdoor datebook or visit its website at http//www.tpwd.state.tx.us. There are clickable maps, as well as the outdoor datebook and information on hunting, fishing, birding, and tours. There's even a special section just for kids with changing activities and loads of information that is fun to access and is great for school reports. Kids can listen to native animal sounds, read about dinosaurs, or download coloring pages. The page also keeps children abreast of educational events, contests, and recreation opportunities in state parks, including special Halloween and Christmas celebrations.

National Parks

The national park system maintains both historical parks and those dedicated to preserving nature. Big Bend National Park is by far the largest, covering more than 800,000 acres in rugged west Texas. Facilities and accommodations vary with each park. Check the listings in other chapters for specific activities in national parks, or call or write the one you wish to visit.

Amistad National Recreation Area [SP]
Superintendent
P.O. Box 420367
Del Rio, TX 78842-0367
512-775-7491

Big Bend National Park [BB]
Superintendent
Texas 79834
915-477-2251

Guadalupe Mountains National Park [BB]
Superintendent
HC 60, Box 400
Salt Flat, TX 79847-9400
915-828-3251

Padre Island National Seashore [GC]
Superintendent
9405 South Padre Island Dr.
Corpus Christi, TX 78418-5597
512-949-8068

Texas Forests

While children aren't likely to roam forests on their own, national and state forests are a wonderful destination for family and group outings. Texas has four national forests administered by the US Forest Service, and all are located in the eastern Piney Woods section of the state. The forests allow primitive camping except where posted otherwise. Hunting and fishing is regulated by Texas Parks and Wildlife. Facilities and fees for usage vary.

The five state forests are managed by the Texas Forest Service, a part of the Texas A&M University system. There is no overnight camping in state forests, nor is hunting permitted, although fishing is allowed in specified areas. Some forests have nature trails, picnic tables, and other amenities. For more information, contact the individual forests and look for other information in listings in this book.

National Forests

Angelina National Forest [PW]
Forest Supervisor
P.O. Box 756
Lufkin, TX 75901
409-634-7709

Davy Crockett National Forest [PW]
US Forest Service
1240 East Loop 304
Crockett, TX 75835
409-544-2046

Sabine National Forest [PW]
Ranger, Tenaha District
101 S. Bolivar
San Augustine, TX 75972
409-275-2632

Sam Houston National Forest [PW]
Raven District Office
P.O. Box 393
New Waverly, TX 77358
409-334-6205

State Forests

Fairchild State Forest [PW]
409-273-2261

Jones State Forest [PW]
214-657-0511

Kirby State Forest [PW]
409-283-3785

Masterson State Forest [PW]
409-283-3785

Siecke State Forest [PW]
409-283-3785

Traveling Texas Roads

The Lone Star state has one of the most extensive and finest highway systems in the United States. Generally the roads are wide and often straight and flat, with adequate shoulders for emergencies. The Texas Department of Transportation maintains rest stops, some with picnic areas and restrooms.

Texas law requires front-seat passengers in cars and light trucks to wear seat belts. All children under age 4 must be secured regardless of where they sit, and those ages 2 to 4 can use seat belts or a federally approved child safety seat. Children under 2 must travel in a federally approved seat. By law, motorcycle drivers and passengers no longer need wear helmets, although it is advised that they do so.

Once you have determined your destination in Texas, you can get a list of accommodations and local attractions, as well as news about the area and the best route there by calling a Texas Travel Counselor from the Texas Department of Transportation at 1-800-452-9292. Tell them where you are heading and they can answer your questions. They will also send you a copy of the *Texas State Travel Guide,* the *Official Texas Map,* the *Texas Events Calendar,* and the *Texas Accommodations Guide* for free!

Climate

Summer sinks in deep in all parts of Texas, with plenty of sun for outdoor fun. Unfortunately, the preponderance of sun can also result in overexposure to the sun's harmful rays. In fact, Texas ranks only behind California in the number of cases of skin cancer in the United States. It pays to use sunscreen when hiking, swimming, or participating in any outdoor activity, no matter what the season. Hats, cover-ups, and quality sunglasses for kids are also a good idea. Inland temperatures, particularly in the southwest, can soar to dangerous highs in the summer. Take shade in the afternoon and drink plenty of fluids.

Fall may be the loveliest time of year in Texas. The days are generally warm to cool and the nights crisp. Like other states, the leaves in Texas change color as cool weather settles in, although the season runs behind that in northern states. This is a great time for children to move to the outdoors, although they may need a light jacket at night.

Cold fronts often blow completely through the state, but winters are mild compared with the rest of the country and generally start late and end early. Naturally winters are milder in the southern part of the state and along the Gulf Coast, where seasons can pass without a freeze. Occasional snow and ice are real possibilities in the panhandle region and upper plains. Traveling during an ice or snow storm can be hazardous and frustrating, since Texans aren't really geared up for this kind of weather on a regular basis. It isn't odd to see schools and businesses shut down and roads closed due to an unusual ice or snow storm, and Dallas/Fort Worth airport can quickly fill up with stranded travelers waiting for delayed flights and for planes to de-ice.

Spring is a blooming good time to be in Texas, as the roadsides and fields fill with wildflowers. The days are often warm and clear, while the nights remain cool, with stray cold fronts that may bring heavy rain, wind, and dramatic lightning shows. College students and families often hit the Gulf beaches and other watering holes during spring break—usually in March. On the coast, though, this can be an "iffy" time of year, with cloudless days and 80-degree temperatures one day and cold fronts, cloudy skies, rain, and 50-degree temperatures the next.

Hurricane season runs from June through November. Today, there is always a good deal of advanced warning should a storm develop or move into the Gulf, so that travelers can alter their plans. The best course of action is simply to keep an eye on the coast and an ear to the weather station during this time and heed the warnings.

Texas records the greatest number of tornadoes in the United States—about 15–20 percent of approximately 1,000 storms per year. However, when that number is compared with land mass,

Texas moves to ninth place. Most tornadic action occurs in northern Texas, in the panhandle region across to Dallas and east Texas. Tornadoes often precede or accompany cold fronts in spring.

Kids' Wilderness Survival

Parents who travels to forests, parks, or wilderness areas have likely thought about the possibility of their child wandering off and getting lost. There is no horror quite so profound as realizing a child is missing. Unfortunately, the panic both adults and children feel in this predicament often causes them to do things to make the situation even more serious.

The purpose of a wilderness survival class is to teach children and parents or adult leaders what to do if children get lost or separated from the family or group in the outdoors. One program that is aimed specifically at children is the "Hug-a-Tree" course, which began in California. The goal of this program is to teach kids not only how not to get lost, but how to stay comfortable if they do, and how to better their chance of getting spotted and rescued. Hugging a tree means sticking next to a tree so that the child is stationary and has cover from the elements. There are six other principles that are included in the program, along with tips for both kids and adults.

The program approaches the dilemma of "being lost" from a child's perspective and addresses common fears that often prevent children from being rescued. For instance, children who may be lost in the woods at night are often afraid of animals and hide from noises. Instead of encouraging them to remain quiet and hide, the course teaches them to yell if they hear a noise. Wild animals will almost certainly run away, and the noise the child hears may well be a rescuer, and their yelling will attract attention.

The program is short and comes with handouts. It is a wonderful general safety education course or a preparatory one if a school or youth group is preparing a field trip into a wilderness area or park. Ask your local search-and-rescue team if they offer a similar class. If there is not program in your area or you want more information on the Hug-a-Tree program, or wish to schedule it in your area, contact:

Hug-a-Tree Program
Jacquelyn Beveridge
6465 Lance Way
San Diego, CA 92120
619-286-7536
or
TPW—Training Program
Public Lands Division
4200 Smith School Rd.
Austin, TX 78744
512-389-4477

Many of the state parks give survival classes at various times of the year, but there are no selected parks that guarantee to offer a course. To see which parks are offering a course, parents or kids need to check the *Texas Parks & Wildlife* magazine outdoor datebook or the TPW website at http//www.tpwd.state.tx.us.

Curricula and strategies will vary with the training and teaching style of the park rangers or volunteers, and with the park geography as well. Classes will generally require kids to be accompanied by a parent, and run about three hours. State parks that offered kids' survival programs in the past include:

Choke Canyon State Park
512-786-3868

Cleburne State Park
817-645-4215

Keechi Creek WMA in Leon County
903-389-2216

Richland Creek Wildlife Management area near Fairfield
903-389-2216

Chapter Two

Places with Great Programs for Kids

Texas has many wonderful zoos, aquariums, nature centers, and museums, but the ones in this section make an effort to go beyond a "walk-and-view" format. They have well-developed hands-on programs for children and a demonstrated dedication to passing on knowledge about native flora and fauna and state geography and geology to the next generation.

Armand Bayou Nature Center [GC]
5600 Bay Area Boulevard
Houston, TX 77258
281-474-2551

This 2,000-acre preserve contains forest, marsh, and prairie located in the Clear Lake Area. It offers hiking trails and boating, and staff members teach year-round classes for youngsters ages 4 through 17. Activities include exploring forests and prairies, setting up an aquarium, collecting live specimens, and tracking. Tuition for classes varies. Members receive a discount. The center is open Wednesday through Sunday and admission is free.

Each summer the center presents an Eco-Camp for boys and girls ages 5 through 10. There are typically two sessions, one in June and the other in July, and children can go half-day or all day.

The EcoCamp activities include hiking, nature study, and scavenger hunts.

The center also sponsors an Adventure Camp for children 9 and 10 years old. Campers can expect a week of boating, canoeing, exploring, and outdoor cooking. There is even one overnight camp-out. Camp sessions last one week and run from 9:00 A.M. to 3:00 P.M. The cost is $150 for members and $200 for non-members.

Austin Nature Center [HC]
301 Nature Center Drive
Austin, TX 78746
512-327-8181

This wonderful center, part of Austin's Park & Recreation Department, is strongly dedicated to kids and families, providing ongoing programs and classes for preschoolers through teens. Preschoolers can attend the Nature's Way Preschool and learn about nature, science, and the environment. The preschool meets two days a week from 9:00 A.M. to 1:00 P.M. and costs $100 a month. Children may join the "Kids and Critters" for $25 or $35 per family and receive a newsletter three times a year, along with discounts on birthday parties and store purchases. Members also get priority during summer-camp registration.

In the summer, youngsters may sign up for day camp for kids ages 3 through 12, centered around a particular outdoor/nature theme. Examples from previous camps include Texas Habitats, Fossil Finders, and Wet, Wonderful Water. Prices, times, and topics vary, so call for a current schedule. The Austin Nature Center is located in Zilker Park next to Town Lake, Barton Springs Swimming Hole, and Zilker Botanical Gardens.

Cibolo Wilderness Trail and Nature Center [HC]
1 mile east of Main Street outside of Boerne on Hwy. 46
Friends of the Cibolo Wilderness

Box 9
Boerne, TX 78006
210-249-4616

Fired by the initiative of self-taught naturalist Carolyn Chipman-Evans, local citizens turned a once neglected and abused piece of land into an award-winning nature area and center. The community of Boerne has put countless hours into improving this 75-acre complex that offers a natural get-away with numerous educational opportunities for all age groups, including kids.

The Cibolo Kids Club, for children ages 3 through 11, meets here once a month for crafts, outdoor activities, and puppet shows. Older middle and high school kids can join the Cibolo Trailblazers and participate in activities that blend outdoor fun with community service, with activities such as camping trips and river clean-up campaigns. In the summer, the center hosts a Nature Adventure Day camp open to 5- through 12-year-olds. The camp runs half a day and deals with nature study and appreciation.

The center also works with area public schools, supplying facilities and materials to integrate into various subjects. The SEED program (Self Esteem through Ecological Dynamics) is a unique effort especially for kids with behavioral or emotional problems. The children work on outdoor projects under the supervision of a social worker to gain self-esteem and respect.

Dallas Museum of Natural History [PL]
P.O. box 150349
Dallas, TX 75315
214-421-3466

The mission of this museum is to focus on the natural history of specimens native to Texas. Exhibits include both past and present animal and plant life displayed in over 50 dioramas, representing major habitats of Texas from the coast to the Chihuahuan Desert. The museum also showcases traveling exhibits, fossils, and fossil life of Texas, along with animals constructed from real bones, including a sea turtle, a mammoth, and various dinosaurs.

Kids enjoy the interactive wet cave made of concrete which simulates animal life in wet caves of Texas. In the basement, children can watch through a window as the fossil preparator reconstructs dinosaurs in the lab. Another favorite with kids is the "Six Legs Over Texas" program, in which teenage interpreters explain insects to children and even let the kids hold some of the live specimens.

The museum gives tours and programs to schools across the state on a variety of topics—the favorite being Texas dinosaurs. The museum will visit schools that are too far to travel with its traveling outreach program.

Finally, during holidays and the summer, through its day camps, the museum provides enlightening and entertaining programs for children about natural history and science. Students enjoy the Lagoon Program, where they take water samples and analyze them or trap tadpoles and minnows from the museum's Lea and Hart Lagoon. The summer camp lasts one week, runs from 9:30 A.M. until 3:00 P.M., and costs $90.

The museum is open daily from 10:00 A.M. to 5:00 P.M. Children ages 3 to 18, along with senior citizens, pay a $2.50 admission fee. Children under 2 are admitted free of charge. All others pay $4.

Dallas Nature Center [PL]
7171 Mountain Creek Parkway
Dallas, TX 75249
214-296-1955

This 630-acre wilderness preserve is just 20 miles from downtown Dallas on White Rock Lake. The site is located on one of the biggest fossil beds in Texas, which makes it a naturally great

place for kids to study fossils. Families can hike nine nature trails through the native vegetation typical of what once covered the north-central plains. Children will enjoy the guided trail walks, along with a scavenger hunt.

The center is committed to children's education and holds in-house and outreach classes and clinics on topics such as animal tracking, pond study, insects, and nature survival. It has a special preschool program as well, and will adapt materials at any level to a youth group. In addition, it will work with teachers and group leaders to develop a class around a new topic. In the spring, it hosts the Great American Birdhouse and Wildflower Festival, when children have the opportunity to build birdhouses and practice nature photography.

Classes at the center should be booked at least two weeks in advance and are offered year-round. In-house classes cost $3 per person, with a minimum of 10 children. One adult per 10 children is required. Outreach classes run $2 per person, with a $50 minimum. Trails are open daily during daylight hours and admission is free. The nature center is open from 10:00 A.M. until 2:00 P.M., Tuesdays through Sundays.

Fort Worth Museum of Science and History [PL]
1501 Montgomery Street
Fort Worth, TX 76107-3079
817-732-1631

Step into the past when dinosaurs ruled Texas at this museum's "Dino Dig" exhibit. Kids can become paleontologists for a day and dig for dinosaur bones outside in a special area. There is also a gallery with rocks and fossils, and there are two life-sized dinosaurs which guard the digging area outside the museum.

Kids will enjoy the hands-on exhibits, including a chance to try on a pair of western chaps. The facilities also include the Noble Planetarium and Omni Imax theater. Admission is $3 for children ages 3–12 and $5 for those older, as well as adults. Seniors pay $4. The museum is open daily, except for Thanksgiving, Christmas Eve, and Christmas.

Houston Arboretum & Nature Center [GC]
4501 Woodway Dr.
Houston, TX 77024
713-681-8433
Fax: 713-681-1191

The Houston Arboretum encompasses over 150 acres of nature, with winding trails and pleasant stops along the way. Check out the special guided and self-guided tours just for kids. Take part in the Arboretum Amble and two-mile pledgewalk along the park's *Out Loop*. All funds raised in the walk go to educational programs at the center.

There is a special botanical hall for children at the Houston Arboretum, and the Learning Tree is a popular attraction with kids. The Learning Tree is a mock-up of a giant oak tree, only big enough for several people to fit inside. Children can push a button and learn about photosynthesis or find out how trees feed and shelter animals. Children's programs at the center run year-round. A sampling includes two two-hour programs for 5- through 12-year-olds entitled "Saturday Happenings" and "Summer Nature Discovery." "Tyke Hikes" for preschoolers takes place on Tuesday afternoons during the summer. Children must be accompanied by a parent on these nature hikes. With free admission and open daily from 8:30 A.M. to 6:00 P.M., the Houston Arboretum is a great bargain.

Houston Museum of Natural Science [GC]
One Hermann Circle Drive
Hermann Park
713-639-4629
Houston, TX 77030

The Houston Museum of Natural Science sponsors a vast array of children's programs, from Gulf coast ecology study to bird watching and ornithology. Kids may investigate the history of sharks, the rainforest, or a particular biological niche. The museum's "Wildlife on Wheels" is a special outreach program that brings a zoologist into public schools to talk to students about wildlife and animals.

In its X•Plorations summer program, the museum offers over 100 classes and camps for children 4 to 12 years of age, dealing with every imaginable nature subject. They last one week, from Monday to Friday, and run from 10:00 A.M. until 3:00 P.M. Field trip camps, for 10- to 12-year-olds, are very popular and fill up fast. They run from 9:00 A.M. until 4:30 P.M. The "Coastal Ecology" trip takes kids to Bolivar Island off Galveston to observe and study coastal life, and a new trip called "On the Road Again" transports students to a new site every day, such as the George Observatory and the Houston Ship Channel. Camp sessions cost between $55 and $130, depending on the subject and age group. Call or write for a current schedule and reservations. The center is open from 9:00 A.M. and 6:00 P.M. Monday through Saturday and 11:00 A.M. to 6:00 P.M. on Sunday. Group discounts are available.

Lubbock Lake Landmark State Historical Park [PP]
Park Superintendent
P.O. Box 2212
Lubbock, TX 79408-2212
806-765-0737
806-741-0306

There isn't a lake anymore at Lubbock Lake Landmark Historical Park, and oddly, that's a good thing. In the early 1900s, the lake was a water source for Lubbock. As water use increased, the lake dried up, and workers dredged the lake bed. Two teens then discovered ancient bones and a projectile point which dated back 10,500 years. Since that time, archeologists have determined that humans lived at this site as far back as 12,000 years.

This 300-acre archeological preserve, along with the Robert A. Nash Interpretive Center, offers a wide variety of educational programs and opportunities for children and adults. The site has two interpretive trails and a four-mile nature trail, and the center includes exhibits and life-size dioramas that explain the transition of plants, animals, and humans through years of climatic changes.

The center encourages hands-on participation by letting kids explore the "Education Collection" of points, bones, and tools. The tour includes demonstrations of site-mapping, excavations, and analysis. Children may also try their hand at bead-working, flint-knapping, pottery-making, and hide-tanning. Kids will marvel at the life-size bronzes of an extinct giant armadillo, a short-faced bear, and an ancient bison that sit around the exterior of the center. The park is open Tuesday through Saturday from 9:00 A.M. until 5:00 P.M., and Sunday from 1:00 to 5:00 P.M.

Moody Gardens [GC]
One Hope Blvd.
Galveston, TX 77554
409-744-1631
1-800-582-4673

The Moody Gardens on Galveston Island give kids a chance to experience a side of nature they might not otherwise encounter. It's best recognized for its five-story glass pyramid which houses a rainforest with ponds, tropical fish, and wading birds. Kids will enjoy the Bat Cave, with a resident colony of 60 fruit bats, and the Butterfly Hatching Hut, where they can watch butterflies emerge and flutter into the giant glass pyramid.

The Moody Gardens offers a nice selection of programs for children during the school year and summer. The gardens run environmental workshops in the Rainforest Overlook on subjects such as recycling and bayou animals. In addition, there are Earth Fair Workshops hourly on herb gardening, tropical plants, and Gulf Coast wildflowers.

The summer ushers in Explorer's Apprentice Summer Camp. Children in grades 3 through 5 attend day camp from 9:00 A.M. to 3:00 P.M. each day and explore the environment with a variety of fun activities.

Nature Discovery Center [GC]
7112 Newcastle
Belaire, TX 77402
713-667-6550

This nature center offers an extensive list of summer classes and day camps. Students in primary grades might investigate wetland life using games and puzzles, while older kids hone mapping and orienteering skills or gather data and perform experiments. Call or write for a schedule and class fees.

Other ongoing activities at the center include family nature rambles and nature story time for preschoolers. There are also ecology exhibits and other displays to view and explore. Children under 10 must be accompanied by an adult. The center charges no admission fee but accepts donations. It's open every day except Monday and Friday.

San Angelo Nature Center [PP]
7409 Knickerbocker Road
San Angelo, TX 76904
915-942-0121

The small nature center houses both live and taxidermic animal species indigenous to the Concho Valley and Edwards Plateau. What makes it uniquely special is that children may hold and pet most of the live animals, including snakes, possums, rabbits, hedgehogs, and rodents. Another strength of the center lies in its programs geared specifically for kids. The museum has developed two curriculum units, one on animals of the region and the other on water using the native wetlands, for elementary schools. The center staff will also work with schools to develop and deliver specific programs, including two popular ones on bats and snakes.

In the summer, this center, located on Lake Nasworthy, opens two weeks for nature day camp in week-long sessions. It also fea-

tures two trail complexes—one that is a one-mile hike and another that is made up of seven miles of trails. Summer hours run from 10:00 A.M. to 3:00 P.M., Wednesday through Sunday, and winter hours are 1:00 P.M. to 6:00 P.M. Admission is $1 for children 12 and under and $2 for older kids and adults.

> The San Antonio Botanical Center [HC]
> 555 Funston
> San Antonio, TX 78209
> 210-207-3250
> Educational Director—Elizabeth Hughes

Located in the Lucille Halsell Conservatory, this center offers seasonal flower exhibits amid a tumbling waterfall. Venture outside and wander among the 45 acres of native Texas flora set in natural environments. Each section is devoted to a different vegetative region: East Texas, Southwest Texas, and the Hill Country. Children will enjoy the pioneer cabins the center moved in, restored, and placed amid the native plants. Each is typical of the region: a smokehouse in the East Texas area, an adobe cabin in the Southwest section, and a stone house in the Hill Country region.

Children have their own garden at the center, and 120 kids meet each Saturday to practice organic vegetable gardening and take home their goodies. From September to May, children can take nature and craft lessons at the gardens for $10 per lesson. The summer is dedicated to Nature Camp, a time to get wet and dirty. Kids sign up for one-week sessions that last half a day. They use the garden's plants, lily pond, and small lake to study subjects such as insects, birds, aquatic life, and gardening. Every day they bring home a nature craft, perhaps a pressed plant or a mobile with different types of bats. The camp costs $55 per week, but over half of the campers are on scholarships funded by the San Antonio Junior League.

Schools can call for group tours or information about the Terrarium Program. Through this program, classes study plants around the world, the water cycle, and the carbon cycle. At the end of the class, students build terrariums to take back to school. The gardens are open from 8:00 A.M. to 5:00 P.M. Monday through Sunday. Admission is only $1 for children 3 through 13 and $4 for teens and adults. Group rates are 50 cents for children age 3–13 and $2 for teens.

Texas State Aquarium [GC]
Corpus Christi Beach
P.O. Box 331307
Corpus Christi, TX 78463
512-881-1200 or 1-800-447-GULF

The Texas State Aquarium is located on 7.3 acres on Corpus Christi Beach. Its focus is plant and animal life indigenous to the Gulf of Mexico, which it celebrates in exhibits that duplicate and explore local ecosystems. Exhibits include more than 250 species in over 350,000 gallons of water. Children like to pick up and pet live specimens at the "Sea Star Discovery Pool" and the "Touch of Adventure," a 5,000-gallon tank featuring small stingrays and sharks where young visitors can actually touch the specimens without being harmed. The sea otters are probably the biggest hit with kids, with their marvelous acrobatic moves both in and out of the water, and the kids really gather around when the staff feeds them.

The aquarium offers reduced admission fees for children and ten-cent Tuesdays in the summer, allowing children to tour the premises for only a dime when accompanied by an adult. Programs include school and youth group tours, lessons during the year, Seaside Saturday classes, Sea-Schooler for preschoolers, and an annual otters' Christmas party. Children who join the aquarium can use the Weston's Library, stocked with books and materials and a computer with Internet access.

SeaCamp is marine science summer day camp for kids ages 6 through 15. Junior SeaCamp is for the younger set up to 8 years old. They learn about the marine world with fun activities like fish printing, indoor canoeing, and making fishing poles. Regular SeaCamp is for children 9 through 12. Campers keep aquariums, canoe inside and out, and spend one night sleeping at the aquarium. Older students with SeaCamp experience take SeaCamp II. These campers perform actual field work, and canoe and sleep-over one night.

SeaCampers can now take computer camp as well, which allows them use of the Weston's Library and computer to create multimedia presentations on marine animals. The camps cost $65 to $85, with a $10 discount for members.

Chapter Three

Fishing & Shooting Sports

Fishing and hunting are Texas traditions that date back to the times when Texans lived off the land by growing produce and harvesting fish and game for food. Although fishing and hunting are not likely our sole means for survival today, these sports compel us to step back in time and out of civilization, to slow down and be in tune with the natural world. Fishing and hunting offer a chance for children and parents to escape to the outdoors and experience an adventure together. They are activities that remind us we are a part of nature and the cycle of life.

Fishing

Fishing for some fun? Then you've come to the right state. Along the Texas Gulf Coast there are 250 different species of fish to catch. Popular saltwater catches include the big trio—flounder, spotted seatrout (speckled trout), and red drum (redfish)—along with king mackerel, grouper, red snapper, and black drum. Piers jut out into bays and the Gulf up and down the coast, making fishing with children especially convenient.

Common inland water fish include largemouth, smallmouth, and spotted bass, catfish and sand bass. Some rivers and lakes are also stocked with Florida bass, walleye, rainbow trout, flounder, and striped bass. Check with the individual waterway for restrictions. Some adhere strictly to a catch-and-release program or support Share-A-Lunker, a program that enables fisheries to borrow live trophy Florida bass (13 lbs. or larger) for research and tracking, then release them back into nature. The angler supplying the lunker receives a free replica of the fish.

Kids under 17 do not need a fishing license to fish in Texas, but they must adhere to size and bag limits when fishing. To receive more information about limits and other laws pertaining to fishing on Texas waters, pick up a free fishing guide usually available at local convenience stores, sporting goods stores, and tourist bureaus. To get one through the mail, call the Texas Parks & Wildlife at 1-800-792-1112.

Safe Boating and Water Safety Classes

Whether you're anchoring off an oil rig to snorkel or motoring to your lucky fishing hole on an inland lake, being in and on the water often requires a boat trip. And as more folks venture out on Texas waterways, the more crowded they become and the more likely the chance for boating accidents. Taking a safe boating class is one step in educating children about the rules of the road, basic first aid, and procedures for surviving an accident or emergency on the water.

Texas law requires that children under 13 wear a PFD (personal flotation device) while in motorboats under twenty-six feet that are under way. A logical precaution is to require all children of any age to wear a PFD while in any type of boat. In Texas, children must be at least 13 years of age to operate a vessel on the water. Those under 16 must be accompanied by an adult 18 or older or have passed a boater education course. This applies to operating a windblown vessel over fourteen feet in length, a power boat with more than fifteen horsepower, or a personal watercraft with more than ten horsepower. Boater education classes are open to all ages, but children under 12 should be accompanied by an adult.

United States Coast Guard Auxiliary
United States Coast Guard
Washington, DC 20593-0001
202-267-1077
For boating courses in your area, call 1-800-336-BOAT

The Unites States Coast Guard Auxiliary, a volunteer helping organization of the Coast Guard, conducts safe-boating classes throughout the United States for all ages. Often these trained volunteers go into classrooms at schools or talk to youth groups about water and boating safety. Upon leaving, the kids receive a coloring workbook that reinforces the safety lessons taught. There are three levels of books, geared for lower elementary age children through teens. Each has activities to encourage children to practice safe boating, from wearing a PFD to filing a float plan.

Texas Parks & Wildlife Boater Education Program
4200 Smith School Road
Austin, TX 78744-3292
1-800-792-1112

The Texas parks department offers safe-boating classes that are open to children. Department certified instructors conduct boater safety classes across the state using the US Coast Guard and Power Squadron's courses. The classes emphasize navigation, rules of the road, safety, trailering, and personal watercraft safety. Those who successfully complete the course receive certification and a shoulder patch. The course is free and covers six hours of instruction time.

Fun Fishing Programs

The following programs are designed to introduce kids to the fun of fishing and educate them about fishing in Texas.

KIDFISH
3810 Medical Parkway, Suite 245
Austin, TX 78756
512-419-9400 (phone) or 512-419-7711 (fax)
Director—Jody Jackson

KIDFISH is a recreational and educational fishing tournament currently held in 37 cities across Texas. The program began in Texas in 1994 as a way to introduce the joys of fishing to children throughout the state. Funds from the program come from sponsors and go toward local fishing programs, education, and fishery enhancement. Children do not have to sign up sponsors, however, in order to participate.

KIDFISH is a three-part event. First the kids attend KIDFISH College, which is a short presentation on fishing, ecology, and safety. Next they hit the local designated fishing hole to try their luck. No experience or equipment is necessary. Tackle and bait are provided by the tournament. The event ends with an awards assembly. All children get a goody bag with educational material, prizes, and an event ribbon. T-shirts and additional prizes are usually available for the winning fish and top fundraisers.

National Fishing Week

National Fishing Week is celebrated in the first or second week of June, and many state parks hold special celebrations and contests during this time. During this week, everyone can fish without a license, and adults are encouraged to take advantage of this by going fishing with their children. To celebrate this special week, Matagorda Island State Park waives its $5 fee for ferry rides

and transportation to the beach for children 12 years old and under. The ferry runs from Port O'Connor to the island. Reservations are required. Call 512-983-2215. [GC]

The Kids All-American Fishing Derby
Hooked on Fishing International
Box 691200
Tulsa, OK 74169

Held during National Fishing week in June, this is the world's largest fishing celebration for kids. The derby is sponsored by the American Fishing Tackle Manufacturers' Association and is conducted in parks and recreation areas.

Hooked on Fishing—Not on Drugs
Route 1, Box 926
Hemphill, TX 75948
409-787-3110
Director—Paul Hinton
Schools wishing to participate can call Holt Taylor
at 1-800-945-6044

This national award-winning program is sponsored by the Future Fisherman Foundation. It combines angler education with drug prevention using community volunteers. The goal is for children to form fishing clubs, receive angler certification, and enjoy doing something useful and wholesome rather than just "hanging out." The program involves school-integrated curricula for grades K through 12 and features poster and essay contests.

The following Texas waters have participated in the "Hooked on Fishing—Not on Drugs" program in the past:

Shirley Creek Marina on Sam Rayburn Reservoir [PW]
409-787-3110

Lake Arlington [PL]
817-451-6860

Pathway to Fishing
USFWS, Superintendent of Documents
202-512-1800
Fax: 202-512-2250

Materials in this package can be used with a school or youth group or along with children's fishing clinics. Students learn about the basics of fishing with posters, scripts, and worksheets. Subjects include casting and fishing techniques and knot-tying. The cost for the packet is $61.

Texas Freshwater Fisheries Center [PL]
5550 Flat Creek Road
Athens, TX 75751
903-676-BASS

This educational center is a combination zoo, laboratory, water-processing plant, and outdoor-fishing experience. For young anglers there is an outdoor two-acre casting pond stocked with 5,000 to 7,000 channel catfish in the summer and rainbow trout in the winter. Kids can get outfitted with fishing equipment from the Angler's Pavilion and try their luck. Wheelchair accessible.

State Parks Fishing Workshops and Tournaments

A vast majority of Texas state parks are situated on an inland body of water and provide good access for family fishing. Many also hold special events or have unique features just for kids. Cedar Hill State Park in northeast Texas, for instance, has a perch pond stocked just for the use of young anglers. For more on this park, contact:

Cedar Hill State Park [PL]
Park Superintendent
P.O. Box 941
Cedar Hill, TX 75104
214-291-3900

Other state parks with lakes sponsor children's fishing rodeos, tournaments, and clinics—some year-round and others in the

spring and summer. Check the outdoor datebook in *Texas Parks &
Wildlife* magazine or the TPW website for current events. The following state parks offered annual kids' fishing tournaments or
workshops at the time of publication. The programs in state parks
are subject to change, though, so always call in advance. For
details, call or write the park superintendent at the address given.
To find out about other parks that may have programs, or for
more information in general, call TPW at 1-800-792-1112.

Kids' Fishing Day—Daingerfield State Park [PW]
Rt. 1, Box 286-B
Daingerfield, TX 75638
903-884-3833

Fishing day is in June from 1:00 to 3:00 P.M. Preschool kids to
12-year-olds can get outdoors and learn about the sport of fishing
and then put their skills to work. All necessary equipment is provided.

Skip-A-Generation Fishing Clinic—
Fairfield Lake State Park [PL]
Route 2, Box 912
Fairfield, TX 75840
903-389-4514

Kids of all ages team up with one of their grandparents and
learn fishing tips and equipment handling. Rangers give demonstrations and share fishing secrets, then everyone fishes off the
pier and at the adjacent cove. A Texas Conservation Passport
(TCP) is required. Call 1-800-792-1112 for more information on
the TCP or see chapter 1, pages 3–4.

Youth Fishing Tournament—
Lake Whitney Youth Fishing Tournament [PL]
P.O. Box 1175

Whitney, TX 76692
817-694-3793

Come join the fun on the first Saturday of June each year as this park celebrates Free Fishing Day in Texas. Kids ages 4 to 12 can compete in a fishing tournament just for them. The park provides equipment, and local bait stands donate bait. Volunteers register kids at 1:00 P.M., and the fishing begins at 2:00 P.M. and ends at 3:00 P.M. Each fish is measured and then released. The angler with the largest number of total inches wins. First- and second-place winners in each of three age divisions receive tackle boxes or rods and reels. Certificates go to the most fish and the biggest fish, and all youngsters receive participation ribbons. Reservations are required, so call ahead of time. There is no fee other than the state park entry or camping fee for adults.

Children's "Perch Jerk" Contest—
Martin Creek Lake State Park [PW]
Route 2, P.O. Box 20
Tatum, TX 75691
903-836-4336

This park has two tournaments—the Perch Jerk on Labor Day weekend and another fishing tournament on Free Fishing Day. The contests are for children age 4–12, divided into age groups: age 4–6, 7–9, and 10–12. Kids must provide their own gear, but bait is available for sale at the park.

The rules require only one pole per person and parents can only bait the hook and remove the fish. All fish are kept alive and released, so bring a bucket. The contest runs one hour, from 2:00 to 3:00 P.M. The child who catches the most fish wins, and a tie is broken by weighing the stringer. Anglers who win first through third prize receive trophies and awards. All kids get a small prize. There is no fee other than the entrance fee for adults of $2.

Parents should register their child 1½ hours before the tournament.

Children's Fishing Derby—
Washington-On-The Brazos State Historical Park [PL]
P.O. Box 305
Washington, TX 77880
409-878-2214

This derby takes place on two Saturdays in May, from 9:00 to 11:00 A.M. Inland Fisheries staff and park rangers sponsor this event for children ages 4–12. Prizes are awarded at the end of each day. A $2 entry fee and reservations are required.

Saltwater Fishing Opportunities

There are several ways children can enjoy fishing on the Gulf Coast. Families down for a visit can bring a boat or rent one and venture into the Intracoastal Waterway, into the many bays along the coast, or out into the open waters of the Gulf of Mexico. Group and individual charter boats and guide services are available also. Write the chamber of commerce for the particular city or town you plan to visit for a list of guides and charter boats.

Of course, you don't even need a boat to fish the coast. Take advantage of the many private and public docks and piers or wade fish in the shallow edges of the bays or along the Laguna Madre. Finally, try surf fishing at the beach for a challenging and often rewarding good time. Look for several days of calm, flat seas.

For kids who want to learn more about saltwater fishing and ecology or who wish to try their luck in a tournament, consider the following Coastal Conservation Association (CCA) programs geared just for children. The CCA was previously divided into regions, including the Gulf Coast Conservation Association. The association changed to the CCA in order to unite the needs of the entire Atlantic and Gulf Coast states. The CCA is a nonprofit organization which, according to its mission statement, exists to "promote the present and future availability of natural resources for the benefit of private citizens."

New Tide—Coastal Conservation Association
CCA Texas State Office
4801 Woodway, Suite 220-W
Houston, TX 77056
713-626-4222

This youth group is a part of the Coastal Conservation Association. Membership is $10 annually for kids under 17. Each child receives a CCA *Rising Tide* newsletter with news and articles about fishing and the environment, an iron-on patch, and a sticker. Members and will be eligible to enter CCA fishing competitions.

StarKids—State of Texas Anglers Rodeo tournament
Coastal Conservation Association
713-626-4222

This popular saltwater tournament has a special division just for kids ages 6 through 10 called StarKids Youth Scholarships Division. The tournament lasts from the end of May to Labor Day. Children must be members of New Tide, pay a $10 entry fee, and follow the same rules as adult participants. The top winners in each of three categories—flounder, sheepshead and gafftop—will receive a $50,000 scholarship. The scholarship winners may use their prize money to attend any accredited Texas college or university full-time for up to five years.

CCA—Take a Kid Fishing Tournament [GC]
136 W. Cotter
Port Aransas, TX 78373
512-749-5252
Contact: Glen Martin

Here's a chance for parents to take their child to a special tournament on the Gulf Coast. This contest takes place in June each year and is for kids ages 4 to 15. The contest is sponsored by local merchants, the Redfish Bay Charter of CCA, and the Port Aransas Boatmen's Association.

Every registrant receives a prize and trophies and other prizes are also given out to winners. The tournament kicks off with a shrimp boil and registration party. Fishing begins the next morning, continuing into that afternoon and ending with a weigh-in. An awards presentation follows, along with a visit from the Texas State Aquarium mobile unit. The registration fee is $10 and entrants are automatically registered as "New Tide" members (see page 37).

Other Fishing Tournaments

Deep Sea Roundup
P.O. Box 501
Port Aransas, TX 78373
512-749-6339
or
Port Aransas Chamber of Commerce
1-800-452-6278

This annual tournament is the oldest one on the Texas Gulf Coast. It's held the weekend after the 4th of July and is open to both offshore and bay-surf anglers. The youth division is for kids up to 16 years old, who may compete for all the trophies. If a youngster's winning results are better than those of an adult in the open division, the child wins both the youth and the open division trophy. Entry fees in the past have run $65 for pre-registration and $75 for registration at the tournament.

The tournament also sponsors a Piggy Perch Tournament that is open to children regardless of whether they are registered in the Roundup. It is a two-day event held at the municipal harbor and is free. There are two divisions: 5 and under and 6 and older. Winners receive rods and reels.

T.I.F.T. (Texas International Fishing Tournament)
P.O. Box 2714
South Padre Island, TX 78597
210-943-TIFT

T.I.F.T. bills itself as wholesome family fun and puts a great deal of emphasis on attracting youngsters. This five-day annual event draws over 1,000 anglers of all ages from toddlers to grandparents. Age divisions start with anglers 7 years old and under and go up to adults. Anglers can fish in the bays or offshore and top winners in each division receive trophies.

Children have their own special day called "Playday," typically held on the Thursday before fishing begins. Kids can enter contests and play land-based games such as the mullet relay, in which four people must run a relay using a live mullet instead of a baton. Registration fees for competitors in the fishing tournament vary with age. In the past, the youngest participants paid $13. The fee covers two dinners and the awards ceremony on Sunday.

Outdoor Expos

Texas Fly-Fishing & Outdoor Show [HC]
Kerrville Convention Visitors Bureau
1700 Sidney Baker, Suite 200
Kerrville, TX
1-800-221-7958
210-792-3535
Bob Miller: 210-895-4348

The Texas Fly-Fishing Show couldn't have a better setting than the beautiful Guadalupe River. The show takes place on a Friday, Saturday, and Sunday each summer in May. Families will enjoy demonstrations, exhibits, and displays, and over 45 different classes are given at every level. Subjects include entomology to fly tying, casting, and kayaking. The basic lessons are suitable for children and most are free. Expect to pay a fee for more advanced classes for experienced older children and adults.

This show has specific programs just for children. The Pathways to Fishing program is sponsored by the San Antonio and Hill Country YMCA, TPW, and Alamo Fly Fishers and is held each day of the show from 10:00 A.M. to 4:00 P.M. It is oriented toward fly-fishing but involves a variety of activities. Kids should wear clothes they can get wet, as the biologist leading the program will have them in and around the river studying nature and fishing. Children may also take an ocean kayak class and practice their new skills in the river. Lifeguards watch the participants and life jackets are provided.

Texas-Mexico Hunting & Fishing Expo—
Coastal Fisheries Area
Call cosponsors: Texas Coastal Conservation Association
713-626-4222
or Texas Parks & Wildlife Department's coastal fishery division
1-800-792-1112.
Summer at various locations

Look for the Coastal Fisheries area at this annual Expo. It is particularly popular with youngsters. Bass tubs come stocked with saltwater fish for those who want to try their luck. For additional fun, kids can try fish printing or marine animal drawing, or they can check out the marine and saltwater touch tanks. Fishing and boating gear is also on display, along with videos on catch-and-release techniques and artificial reefs.

Sportsman's Extravaganza [PW]
Call cosponsors: Texas Forestry Association 409-632-TREE
or Texas Parks & Wildlife Department 1-800-792-1112.

The Sportsman's Extravaganza is an annual event to help fund outdoor and educational projects in East Texas. The highlight of the show is the 4,500-gallon fishing tank, where kids in the past have caught close to 1,000 fish. There are also educational and recreation displays, fishing demonstrations, and boats and sporting goods for window shopping.

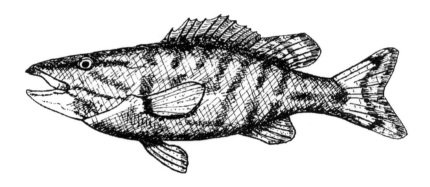

Shooting Sports

Shooting sports offer more to youngsters than a chance to hunt. They improve eye-hand coordination as well as concentration and control. One of the primary benefits kids say they get from shooting sports is social interaction with other children as well as with their own families. Through a well-developed program, children can also learn about gun safety, sporting ethics, and wildlife management.

4H Shooting Sports
Dr. Ron Howard
7607 Eastmark Drive Ste. 101
College Station, TX 77843-2473
409-845-1214

The 4-H Shooting Sports program is the largest and most comprehensive one of its kind for children in Texas. Annually, 7,000 to 10,000 kids participate in 4-H Shooting Sports programs, along with over 2,000 adult volunteers. In addition to developing shooting skills and teaching shooting safety, the 4-H organization aims to encourage children's understanding of natural resources, to enhance self-concept and character, and to strengthen families through recreational activities.

4-H encompasses virtually every shooting activity, including archery, blackpowder, pistol, rifle, shotgun, and hunting and wildlife study. Children may practice or compete in one of the group's many contests throughout the state. For competition, shooters are divided into categories by age: sub-junior, ages 9-12; junior, ages 13-14; and senior, ages 15-18. Participants earn specific patches at each match regardless of their score and some matches award ribbons, medals, plaques, belt buckles, or trophies. Call your local Texas Agricultural Extension Service 4-H for specific programs in a particular area. The office in College Station will also send you a start-up kit to establish a new 4-H Shooting Sports program.

"Five-stand Sporting" Clays—Mobile Shooting Range
Texas Parks & Wildlife Department
4200 Smith School Road
Austin, TX 78744
1-800-792-1112
or
Scotty Oliver
512-389-4572

Sporting clays is a shooting activity similar to skeet shooting in which the shooter uses a shot gun to attempt to hit clay targets thrust into the air. The TPW and the National Sporting Clays Association offers a mobile sporting clays shooting range for hunter education programs around the state. The exhibit is available to youth organizations, including 4-H clubs and Boy and Girl

Scouts for shooting-sports events. Call to book the exhibit or find out more information.

CD Interactive DART
Texas Parks & Wildlife Department
4200 Smith School Road
Austin, TX 78744
1-800-792-1112

High-tech meets high schools and state agriculture science programs through this CD computer player system. The department has an interactive video trailer that is available to groups that teach firearm safety or hunter education courses. Participants "arm" themselves with lasers or arrows and shoot at images of animals or targets on a screen. The system informs the players if their shots are successful or not and how to make better choices next time. Call for availability.

Texoma Lutheran Camp [PL]
Route 1, Box 116-P
Potsboro, TX 75076
903-786-3121
888-886-6198
e-mail: lomtexoma@texoma.net
Director—Keith Lund

During the school year, Texoma Lutheran offers Outdoor Education in one- to five-day camps for schools and youth groups. Teachers select activities and the type of programs to suit their students' needs. Two of the options leaders may choose for their camp are archery and riflery. For more on this camp, see chapter 8.

Hamman Ranch YMCA
Mike Dawson
HC 01 Box 710
Bandera, TX 78003

1-800-531-5694
830-796-7449

Hamman Ranch offers a special adventure camp for youngsters during the summer. Kids can earn their Texas Hunter's Certification at Marksmanship Camp, where they practice with 22's, deer rifles, skeet, blackpowder muzzle loaders, and archery. For more on this camp, see chapter 8.

Hunting

Texas offers a wide variety of game for hunters, including white-tailed deer, mule deer, bobwhite quail, turkey, white-winged doves, ducks, geese, and squirrels.

All hunters are required to purchase a hunting license, regardless of age. Texas residents younger than 17 (along with those older than 64) pay $6 for a Special Resident Hunting license, and residents 17 to 64 pay $19. Non-resident General Hunting licenses cost $250 and allow the hunter to hunt any legal bird or animal except alligators. There are specific licenses for non-residents as well as hunting stamps for specific game or weapons for both resident and non-resident hunters. The archery stamp fee is $7, for example, and a turkey stamp is $5.

In Texas, every hunter born after September 2, 1971 who is age 17 or older must complete a Hunter Education Training Course. This includes out-of-state hunters as well. Those who are ages 12 through 16 must either successfully complete a Hunter Education Training Course or be accompanied by a licensed hunter 17 years of age or older. Children under the age of 12 must be accompanied by a licensed hunter 17 years of age or older.

The cost of certification is $10 and proof of certification must be carried on you as you hunt. For details about hunting regulations, limits, and seasons, pick up a current free hunting guide from Texas Parks & Wildlife (available at many convenience stores, sporting goods stores, and state parks), or call 1-800-792-1112.

The Texas Hunter Education Program

This program is taught by a TPWD-certified hunter education instructor. The class lasts a minimum of ten hours and includes information on hunting safety, rules, ethics, wildlife conservation, different types of sporting arms, and survival and first aid. The program meets the mandatory hunter education requirements for the state. The fee is $5. Upon successful completion of the course, the hunter receives certification and a shoulder patch.

A new alternative to the standard hunter education program is in the works at the Texas Parks & Wildlife Department. Students of all ages can now study at home, taking as much time as they need to master the material before they take a written test. The department supplies students with a field guide, workbook, and video. Once students pass the test, they can finish the program by setting up a hands-on session with trained instructors at various sites around the state. The first such sites will be in the larger urban areas and, as the program progresses, sites will evolve in rural areas. The hands-on approach seeks to give the student real-life training in the field. It involves three sections: 1) skills performed at stations; 2) live firing; and 3) ethics. Call TPW for to find a site in your area and to order materials.

Finding a Place to Hunt

The biggest problem with hunting in Texas might be finding a place to practice the sport. About 97% of Texas land is privately owned, so most hunters pay for a seasonal or daily lease for the right to hunt on a particular piece of private land. To find private land available for lease, try newspaper ads or referrals from other hunters. The *Hunting Clearinghouse Directory* is also available free from the Texas Department of Agriculture at P.O. Box 12847, Austin, TX 78711. Also helpful is the free *Texas Deer Hunting Lease Register* from the Texas Wildlife Association, at 210-826-2904.

Hunting in State Parks & Wildlife Areas

There are over 40 Texas state parks and wildlife management areas available for hunting each season, and many are set aside strictly for youth accompanied by a guardian. Each hunt is categorized by location, type of weapon, and type of game. For instance, a youngster may apply for a shotgun-only hunt or one just for alligators or javelinas. The hunts are determined through a drawing. Some hunts are more popular than others, making the odds of winning some slimmer. For a list of opportunities and an application, call 1-800-7792-1112 or go by a Texas Parks & Wildlife office by July 15. Kids can also visit the TPW home page on the Internet and print off an application. The website address is: http://www.tpwd.state.tx.us.

Texas Youth Hunting Association
Texas Parks & Wildlife
4200 Smith School Road
Austin, TX 78744
1-800-792-1112

The Texas Youth Hunting Association was founded in 1996 with the goal of producing more affordable opportunities for children to hunt in Texas. The organization offers 14 or more youth hunts a year. Members are entered in a pool, and hunts are determined by drawing members' names. Kids who join pay a $5 fee and receive a hat and patch. Regardless of age, members must have passed the Texas Hunter Education Program. The Texas Youth Hunting Association also serves as a clearinghouse, matching youths with other hunting opportunities across the state.

Texas Wildlife Association
1635 N.E. Loop 410, No. 108
San Antonio, TX 78209
210-826-2904

The Texas Wildlife Association is a nonprofit organization dedicated to hunting, fishing opportunities, and land management. The Texas Wildlife Association offers special memberships to children. The Youth Level is for youngsters through 7th grade. They receive a special quarterly youth publication. The Student Level is for full-time students from 8th grade through college levels. These members may attend meetings but cannot vote. The association offers youth hunts to its members. Call for details and see chapter 7, page 117, for information on the association.

The Parrie Haynes Camp

This week-long camp gives underprivileged children a chance to get outdoors and learn to hunt. The camp includes hunter education training, along with other activities. For more about the camp, see chapter 8, page 146, or call 409-345-3562.

Operation Orphans
P.O. Box 535
Mason, TX 76856
915-347-6745
Supervisor—Lyla Croch

Game warden Gene Ashby started this program in 1960 to offer orphaned children a chance to get outdoors and hunt. The program now extends to children in foster homes and group homes. The camp likes to take a group from one home or area for this weekend hunt and tries to contact as many homes as possible across the state. Kids can participate in four white-tailed deer hunts (boys only), an exotic hunt in February, and a girls-only hunt Thanksgiving weekend.

Kids check in Friday night and go through orientation, then relax in the recreation area, playing basketball or shooting pool. The young hunters are in bed by 10:00 P.M. and up by 2:00 or 3:00 A.M. to eat and divide up in groups. Local landowners in the area allow the kids to hunt on their land and harvest excess deer. Hunts use one guide per child for safety reasons and to promote a bonding atmosphere. All guides are required to pass the hunter safety course, and children handle low-caliber guns only when it is time to shoot.

During the hunt, the camp provides meals and donates necessary clothes such as jackets and boots from a stock it collects throughout the year. The home gets to take back any meat the kids shoot. Interested directors of group homes should call to make reservations. Donations of clothing or other goods are always appreciated. Call for more information.

❧

Chapter Four

In & On the Water

Nothing is as refreshing on a hot summer day as taking part in fun in the water. For children who like to get wet, there are plenty of opportunities in Texas. The Lone Star state has 4,790 square miles of inland waters, including 80,000 miles of rivers. Add to that 624 miles of shoreline along the Gulf of Mexico, which includes almost 4 million acres of bays, lagoons, estuaries, and water out into the Gulf of Mexico stretching 9 nautical miles.

Of course, being in and on the water presents obvious hazards. For this reason, it just makes sense to ensure that children can swim well before they participate in water-related activities. Most communities offer swimming lessons. Check with the local Red Cross, city parks and recreation department, YMCA, or YWCA. See chapter 3 for information about safe-boating classes and laws concerning personal flotation devices (PFDs) for children.

Snorkeling and Scuba Diving

Snorkeling is a safe way for kids to see the world beneath the water's surface. Many people associate snorkeling with a trip to the Caribbean or Mexico, but there are many freshwater and salt-water opportunities to snorkel in Texas.

Snorkeling Classes—Houston Scuba Academy
14609 Kimberly at Dairy Ashford
713-497-7651
and
12505 Hillcroft
713-721-7788

For an adventure underwater, children ages 4 to 15 can sign up for private or group snorkeling lessons at Houston Scuba Academy. The academy gives instruction in a swimming pool and follows up the class with educational videos. Classes take place each Saturday from 10:00 A.M. until noon, and the cost is $25. Bring your own gear.

Scuba

Teens may eventually want to try their hand at scuba diving. Of course, scuba diving presents certain hazards that snorkeling doesn't. The industry standard is that children under twelve shouldn't dive because their bodies are still forming, and the compression divers experience may cause physical damage. For teens and adults, diving classes are available at dive shops throughout the state, and shops will generally offer equipment rentals as well. Coastal shops often plan diving trips into the Gulf and to more exotic locations. Check the phone book or look into the local YWCA or YMCA. These agencies offer reasonably priced diving lessons, too.

Freshwater Snorkeling and Diving

All of the clear lakes throughout the state are good freshwater sources for snorkeling and diving. The Hill Country, with its many crystal-clear lakes fed by springs, is a particularly popular area. The following are good bets for snorkeling or scuba diving in fresh water.

Blue Lagoon [PW]
16405 Wall St.
Houston, TX 77040
713-376-3157

This turquoise lagoon has been called "the Texas Cozumel," named after the famed diving water near the Mexican island of Cozumel. The lagoon is really two lagoons on six acres of land in the eastern piney forest area. The low pH (meaning that the water is relatively acid) keeps the water clear so that no algae, or fish for that matter, can live, so don't expect to spot any. There are sunken boats and rock formations, and the visibility is about forty feet. The water temperature swings from the upper forties in the winter to the lower nineties in August.

Swimming and cliff jumping are not allowed, and no children under 12 or pets are admitted. For teens serious about experiencing open-water diving, though, this is an excellent place to learn. Classes are held here and local dive clubs frequent the lagoons.

Lake Amistad [SP]
Chamber of Commerce
1915 Avenue F
Del Rio, TX 78840

Lake Amistad is set in the west Texas scrub of prickly pear and mesquite, and is the result of the damming of the Rio Grande. The lake cuts into the land in inlets and is popular with divers and snorkelers, especially in the fall, winter, and early spring.

San Marcos River [HC]
San Marcos Convention and Visitors' Bureau
P.O. Box 2310
San Marcos, TX 78667
512-396-2495 or 1-800-782-7653 ext. 177

Starting in San Marcos, this river by the same name runs southeast until it joins with the Guadalupe River near Gonzales. The San Marcos River is clear, with an average chilly temperature of 71 degrees. It has twenty-five species of rooted plants and over fifty species of fish, and is home to rare animals, including the fountain darter and the San Marcos salamander.

San Solomon Springs [BB]
Balmorhea State Recreation Area
Box 15
Toyahvale, TX 79786
915-375-2370

Located in the Chihuahuan Desert, this 1.75-acre oasis is the largest manmade pool in the United States. The water is fed by the San Solomon and is replenished naturally at a rate of 26 million gallons per day. The cool, 76-degree water is crystal clear, with a visibility range of 40 to 80 feet. Expect to see catfish, sunfish, turtles, and uncommon species like the Pecos gambusia and the mosquito fish.

Snorkeling and River Hydrographics—
Guadalupe State Park [HC]
Rt. 4 Box 2087
Bulverde, TX 78163
210-438-2656

Learn about the Guadalupe River underwater. Bring your snorkel, your mask, your fins, and your kids and take part in this fun, educational excursion in June from 1:00 to 4:00 P.M. Land-based instruction is given first to introduce everyone to the geography, geology, and hydrology of the area. Reservations are available but are not required. The cost is $3 for children 12 and under, and $5 for those older and adults.

Saltwater Snorkeling and Diving

The success of saltwater snorkeling in Texas depends largely on the weather. Windy days stir up the fine bottom sand of the Gulf of Mexico, making visibility poor. This is especially critical in the shallow water immediately along the coastline. Look for several days of light-to-calm winds in a row during the warm months of July, August, and September to plan a snorkeling trip.

The best spots to view fish are off the coast around oil platforms and next to jetties, where you may see urchins, sergeant majors, sea anemones, and triggerfish. Snorkeling or diving near the rigs feels like swimming in a giant aquarium. Kids may see tropical fish along with large fish like kingfish, barracuda, and ling. They may even run into a whale shark, the largest fish in the Gulf and luckily a plankton feeder.

Another popular scuba site is the Freeport Liberty Ship Reef, one of 24 artificial reef sites in the Gulf of Mexico that is suitable for diving. The Freeport Liberty Ship Reef is 33 nautical miles off the coast of Freeport and water depths range from 65 to 110 feet. Expect to see the ship, the *Star Reef,* made of obsolete oil rigs, and a variety of barnacles, corals, sponges, clams, and fishes.

Flower Gardens Banks National Marine Sanctuary [GC]
Write to: 1716 Briarcrest Dr., Ste. 702
Bryan, Texas 77802
409-847-9296
or
National Oceanic Sanctuaries and Reserves Div.
1305 East West Hwy. SSMC-4
Silver Spring, MD 20910

One of the best spots for diving off the Texas Coast is the Flower Gardens Reefs, one of 13 National Marine Sanctuaries, located about 125 miles southeast of Freeport. The Gardens consist of 350 acres of coral reefs and are the most northerly on the North American continental shelf. There are over 170 species of fish and 250 species of invertebrates to observe, along with 80 species of algae and 21 types of coral. And unlike many other reefs around the world, the Flower Gardens are in very good shape, with no noticeable environmental degradation. Experienced divers can take one of the chartered trips that are offered by dive shops up and down the coast. Divers should be certified. Contact your local dive shop for more information.

Surfing

They say if you can surf the Texas Gulf Coast, you can surf anywhere. The reason is that the waves don't often break in nice clean rows. Instead, the peaks shift, and it is difficult to judge where and how the wave will break. Surfers have to paddle back and forth and move quickly to be in position to catch a good wave. Just paddling out, in fact, can be a good aerobic workout, since the waves often crash together, making it difficult to swim out through them.

While the Gulf Coast isn't known as a world-class surfing destination, the waves are definitely rideable, and many people of all ages and walks of life enjoy the sport. The size and quality of the waves of course will vary with the winds, tides, seasons, and action in the Gulf. Despite what many people believe, the surf in the Gulf is not always small, and in fact can be very big at times. The general rule is that the surf gets better the further south you go. South Padre Island is especially known for larger and better quality surf. The areas around jetties and piers generally produce bigger, cleaner waves as well.

Families on vacation who want to try surfing can rent boards on or near the beach at all the major beach resorts up and down the coast. Whether swimming or surfing, parents should watch children closely along the Texas coast. Often there is a strong current at the beach, and in the summer there may be Portuguese man-o-war, jellyfish, and stingrays. Watch for signs posting warnings and carry meat tenderizer to apply to jellyfish stings.

Texas Gulf Surfing Association, Inc.
P.O. Box 113
Huntsville, TX 77342-0113
409-377-5424

Kids serious about the sport of surfing can join the Texas Gulf Surfing Association. This is an organization for surfers of any age, including kids, and it gives surfers the opportunity to compete with others their own age. The association is divided into two districts: the North District, which starts at Highway 45 in Galveston County and extends to Victoria, and the South District, which is everything south of Victoria County.

Membership is $30 for competitive surfers and $10 for noncompetitive members. Contest entrance fees are extra, but they are nominal. Surfers compete in divisions according to age. "Menehunes" are for boys and girls age 12 and under. The Boys' Division is for ages 13 and 14 and the Jr. Men's is for ages 15 to 17. Girls 12 to 17 compete in the Girls' Division. Special divisions include Jr. Longboard and Jr. Bodyboard for kids 17 and under.

Those who accumulate the most points through the contest season will qualify to compete in the Texas State Surfing Championships. Top point winners following this contest will be invited to the United States Amateur Surfing Championships.

WaveRunners [CG]
10752 SPID
Corpus Christi, TX 78418
512-937-9283

This nonprofit, recreational surfing club is headed up by professionals and business owners along the Texas Gulf Coast. The members are surfers who want to promote a positive image of surfing—especially to young people. The club also has a strong commitment to protecting the environment. According to its mission statement, its wish is to promote "projects aimed at educating the public about beach safety, environmental protection and the recreational opportunities on area beaches." It fulfills its mission by heading up clean-up and environmental protection projects and providing a scholarship to a high school surfer each year. Write for more information.

Boogie Bahn—Schlitterbahn [HC]
Schlitterbahn Waterpark
305 W. Austin St.
New Braunfels, TX 78130
210-625-2351

Self-proclaimed "Surfing Capital of Texas," this park's Boogie Bahn is a continuous manmade wave that challenges surfing and bodyboarding enthusiasts. For most of the season, the water flows at about 12 miles an hour, but the wave can move up to 20 miles an hour and be adjusted to up to eight feet in height. Just staying on the wave is extremely tricky, and be warned, those who master the wave won't get an endless ride. Eventually the park employee who controls the Boogie Bahn from the booth will "toss" the surfer off by changing the speed and flow of the water.

In August, Schlitterbahn also hosts the Annual Flow Rider World Bodyboarding Championships, open to both amateurs and professionals.

Phone and Online Surf Reports

Find out if the waves are ripping, peeling, pounding, or flat before you load up the boards and head for the beach. You can get the information by phone or online.

Galveston
Hardcore 409-763-2115
Underground 409-765-1463

Surfside
Breaker Sports 409-233-8308
Cutback 900-CUTBACK

Corpus Christi
Wind & Wave 512-937-WIND
M.D. Surf & Skate 512-949-RIPS

South Padre Island
On the Beach 956-761-1121
Cutback 900-CUTBACK

Texas Waveriders
http//www.portisabel.com/otble

This website offers general information about surfing in Texas, along with links to surf reports and other sites and surfing photos.

Corpus Christi Surf & Wind Report
www.ciris.net/Irncc/wndsrfpg.html

If you're planning a trip to the Corpus Christi area on the coast and want to learn the current wind, water, and surf conditions, you can get that information online. Also available is information about tides, storms, and weather, as well as buoy reports, photos, and links to other wind and surf web sites.

South Padre Island Surf Report
www.portisabel.com/newsurf.html

This neat website offers local surf news at South Padre along with links to other areas. It also features profiles of local surfers, surf photos, and news from local surf shops.

Canoeing and Kayaking

Canoeing and kayaking enthusiasts frequent almost every waterway in the state. Near rivers and lakes there are also liveries that supply rentals, and the employees are local experts who will explain the area waters and provide a map and put-in and take-out services. In addition, these shops may offer lessons and guided tours and suggest campgrounds in the area. A good book that describes the rivers of Texas and that carries advertisements from local liveries is *Texas Rivers and Rapids* by Ben Nolan and Bob Narramore.

To find lessons locally, call the local canoe or sporting goods shop. Medium-to-large cities will have city parks and recreation divisions with summer programs for youths that may also include canoe or kayaking classes. Also look into your local YMCA and YWCA. These organizations often offer these types of lessons, especially in the summer, using their pools as training areas. The Boys and Girls Clubs and other youth groups are other good sources, since they often have water facilities and plan camping and canoeing outings in conjunction with lessons.

A final opportunity for kids to learn and practice kayaking or canoeing is by attending an outdoor exposition. The Texas Wildlife Expo (see chapter 5, page 76) has a special manmade "wet zone" for kids to try out canoeing. The Texas Fly-Fishing & Outdoor Show in Kerrville each summer offers special children's kayaking lessons in the Guadalupe River. For more information on this show, see chapter 3, pages 39–40, or call 1-800-221-7958.

Of course, children should wear personal flotation devices (PFDs) when canoeing and kayaking and even when tubing if they are not strong swimmers. Watersocks, old sneakers, or water sandals are a good idea to prevent cuts and scrapes from rocks, stumps, or debris. Make sure glasses, sunglasses, and hats are secured, and leave wallets and nice watches at home.

Rowing Web Site
http://www.Neosoft.com/~larevalo/hrc

Check out this website for information about canoe or rowing clubs and events across Texas.

Explorers

Explorers is a part of Boy Scouts of America but is not a traditional scouting experience. Businesses, churches, and individuals who want to share and explore in-depth one aspect of life with young people sponsor Explorer Posts. Kids meet regularly but work as a group on one interest, such as sailing or canoeing, rather than earning badges in a variety of subjects as scouts normally do. Explorers is for young people ages 14 to 21, and unlike other Boy Scouts programs, Explorers is open to both boys and girls.

Scouting interests and the degree of activity vary with councils around the state. To find out about Explorers in your area, look for the Boy Scouts of America in your white pages and check under the headings in this book.

The following posts are Explorer Posts associated with the Boy Scouts of America, whose primary thrust is either canoeing or kayaking or both. Others may be set up in different areas of the state, so check with the local Boy Scouts of America office.

Explorer Post 151 [PP]
2008 Bedford
Midland, TX 79701

Explorer Post 425 [PL]
798 Mercedes
Fort Worth, TX 76126

Hill Country Rivers

Hill country rivers, including the San Marcos River, the Blanco, and the Medina, are popular with canoeists and tubing enthusiasts. The Guadalupe River is probably the most frequently visited, however, and like the others it is generally clear and cold even in the summer. Beginners should be cautious on the Guadalupe as it is easy to get caught sideways or up against the trees and many of the drops are more challenging than they may look at first. People dump over at such a rate, in fact, that divers stake out predictable crash sites to scavenge for sunglasses, money, and anything else of value. To find out about these rivers and accommodations in the area, contact the following:

Bandera Chamber of Commerce (Medina River) [HC]
P.O. Box 171
Bandera, TX 78003
830-796-3045

Blanco State Park [HC]
P.O. Box 493
Blanco, TX 78606
830-833-4333

Guadalupe River State Park [HC]
HC 54, P.O. Box 2087
Bulverde, TX 78163
830-438-2656

New Braunfels Chamber of Commerce (Guadalupe River)
  [HC]
P.O. Box 311417
New Braunfels, TX 78131
830-625-2385

San Marcos River [HC]
San Marcos City Park
512-392-8255
or
Convention and Visitors' Bureau
1-888-200-5620 or 512-392-3760

Austin Nature Center Evening Canoeing [HC]
301 Nature Center Drive
Austin, TX 78746
(512) 327-8181

For children ages 8 to 12, the Nature Center provides basic canoe lessons and water-safety instruction on the San Marcos River. Classes are held in April from 5:30 P.M. to 10:30 P.M. and cost $24 per person. All levels are welcome, but participants should know how to swim. Equipment is provided, but kids need to bring water shoes, a flashlight, a water bottle, and a snack. Look for other activities sponsored by the Nature Center in chapter 2, page 14.

Canoe Lessons—Texas State Aquarium SeaLab [GC]
P.O. Box 331307
Corpus Christi, TX 78402
512-881-1204 or 1-800-477-GULF
Contact—Tara Schultz

Brave the rapids—in air conditioning! The Texas State Aquarium offers canoeing lessons during summer camp and in several short sessions during the school year. All campers start their lesson in the indoor SeaLab tank, a round freshwater tank 4 ½ feet deep. Wearing life jackets, the campers learn the basic paddling skills and how to right their craft if it gets swamped. Kids 9 years

old and up venture out to the Rincon Channel behind the
Aquarium's SeaLab to practice their skills in the wild. Also available in June are special "Seaside Saturday" trips outside, yet close
to the Aquarium, especially for children just learning to canoe.
Kids ages 12 to 15 can join an instructor for a two-hour morning
trip into Nueces Bay for wildlife viewing and wet fun on the water.
Both classes cost $5 for members and $8 for nonmembers each.
(For more programs offered at the Texas State Aquarium see
chapter 2, pages 24–25.)

Southwestern Canoe Rendezvous [PW]
P.O. Box 925516
Houston, TX 77292
713-467-8857

This event is billed as the largest gathering of canoeists and
kayakers in the country. It takes place in October on Lake Raven
in Huntsville State Park. The event includes a giant boat and
equipment auction and a freestyle-canoeing exhibition. There are
hour-long lessons that are free and longer clinics and private
instruction for a fee. Part of the profits help the Galveston Bay
Foundation and the Texas River Protection Association.
Participants must pay the park entrance fee, which is $3 per per-
son for kids 13 and up and adults. Younger children get in free.

Texas Water Safari [HC]
P.O. Box 7221
San Marcos, TX 78130

This annual event is often dubbed the "World's Toughest Boat
Race." It's open to anyone, but minors need to present a waiver
from a parent. Be advised this is a grueling, long trip appropriate
only for experienced canoeists and kayakers. The race involves a
410-mile trip down the San Marcos and Guadalupe Rivers to Sea
Drift on the Gulf Coast. With that distance, just finishing is con-

sidered doing well. Any type of hand-propelled craft can be used. The entry fee is $50 and total prizes of up to $6,500 are awarded.

There are other races across Texas and although most are geared for adults, the Texas Canoe Racing Association has established a Junior Division for kids under 16 who wish to race. Children will compete two to a boat, which can be no longer than 17 feet.

Kayak Rodeo [GC]
To register contact:
Naval Air Station Marina
Corpus Christi, TX 78419
512-939-2811
or
Wind & Wave WaterSports
10721 SPID
Corpus Christi, TX 78418
512-937-9283: Frank Floyd
512-939-8827: Mike McClure

The Kayak Rodeo is an annual fun event that takes place on a Saturday and Sunday in June. The rodeo spans the two weekend days at the Naval Air Station Sunfish Beach and on Padre Island at the Holiday Inn. Kids and adults both will love to romp in the water and sand. Sign up for kayak competitions and a beach volleyball competition. The event includes a T-shirt, barbecue lunch, and use of the kayaks. There are awards for the winners and door prizes, too. The early registration fee is $8 and regular registration is $12.

Armand Bayou Nature Center [GC]
5600 Bay Area Boulevard
Houston, TX 77258
713-474-3074

At the Armand Bayou just 29 miles southeast of Houston, you can get away from the big city without going very far. This 2,000-acre reserve is a popular canoeing spot. Pick up a map first at the center, then put in at Bay Area Park and at the NASA Road 1. Canoes are available for members only. Others need to bring their own gear. The center is open Wednesday through Sunday. For more information on the center, see chapter 1, pages 13–14.

Big Thicket National Preserve [PW]
3785 Milam
Beaumont, TX 77701
409-839-2689

Big Thicket is located off Highway 69/2689 in East Texas. There are 90,000 acres of water and land protected from development within this preserve. The land in the preserve is laced with the Neches River and tributary creeks, giving visitors a variety of opportunities to canoe. The Upper and Lower Neches Rivers are particularly recommended. The lower section is good for a family drift, with calm waters banked by cypress trees. The upper section is faster moving, with occasional boulders.

Guided canoe trips are available if you call ahead for reservations. Also ask about workshops on kayaking and canoeing techniques for both the whole family and kids.

Chris's Cruisin' Canoes [PW]
Angelina/Neches Dam Wildlife Management Area
Martin Dies, Jr. State Park
409-384-5231

For a fun family adventure, try Chris's guided tour down the Angelina/Neches River. It's an easy and gentle float down that starts at 8:00 in the morning. The trip costs $50 for two with a canoe rental or $30 for two bringing their own boat. A $10 fee is charged for a third person. Shuttle service is available for $2 per person. Reservations are required.

Sea Rim State Park—Marshland Canoe and Kayak Trips for
 Families or Youth Groups [GC]
P.O. Box 1066
Sabine Pass, TX 77655
409-971-2559

Sea Rim State Park is located on State Hwy 87 on the Gulf Coast southwest of Port Arthur and northeast of Galveston. The park, which is open from 8:00 A.M. to 5:00 P.M. daily, is unique because of its sea-rim marshes. For canoe and kayak enthusiasts, there are canoe trails through the marsh area where boaters can observe and photograph wading birds, raccoons, opossums, minks, and rabbits. Maps of the canoe trails are available at the park's Marshland Unit. Boaters must file a float plan at head-quarters. Don't forget the insect repellent to ward off the mosquitoes.

Devil's Waterhole Canoe Tour—Inks Lake State Park [HC]
Route 2, Box 31
Burnet, TX 78611
512-793-2223

Crystal-clear Inks Lake nine miles west of Burnet is the setting for this family excursion. The trip runs from 4:00 to 6:30 P.M. at various dates from the spring through the fall. The emphasis of the tour is on exploring the geological and natural features and observing local birds. The cost is $3 for children age 12 and under and $5 for adults. TCP members pay $3. Reservations are required.

State Parks that Rent Canoes

The following state parks advertise canoe rentals at their lakes. For more information, call either the individual park or 1-800-792-1112. For camping reservations at any park, call Texas Parks & Wildlife at 1-512-389-8900.

Huntsville State Park [PW]
P.O. Box 508
Huntsville, TX 77340
409-295-5644

Lake Mineral Wells State Park [PL]
Route 4, Box 39C
Mineral Wells, TX 76067
817-328-1171

Lake Texana [GC]
P.O. Box 760
Edna, TX 77957
512-782-5718

Tyler State Park [PW]
Route 29, Box 29030
Tyler, TX 75706
214-597-5538
Available summer months

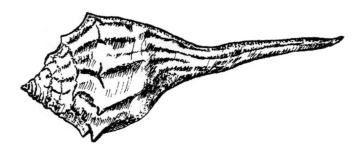

Sailing and Windsurfing

Wind and water—it's the combination necessary for sailing and windsurfing and one that is common across Texas, both inland and on the coast. The mid- to lower Gulf Coast is particularly windy and known worldwide as a hot spot for windsurfing.

The best way to introduce kids to sailing or windsurfing is to enroll them in a class geared for their age. However, you can try both sports by simply renting a sunfish or sailboard. Often shops near lakes and along the coast rent both sailboats and sailboards, and many also offer beginning instruction. Smaller children will need to learn sailing skills on a small boat like an optimist or in pairs on a sunfish. Older children may be able to solo on a sunfish or dolphin. When windsurfing, ask for scaled-down sailboard rigs for children.

Every community large enough to support a yacht club will likely have a junior program in sailing and perhaps even windsurfing for children. These programs will vary, but generally will offer classes, boat storage and rental, and even summer camps. Yacht clubs differ in structure, some being simple and inexpensive, while others may charge very high fees and offer a wide array of services and facilities. If joining a club isn't feasible, it's still worth checking into their summer programs and lessons. Often they are open to the public, or members may be able to sponsor children who aren't members, allowing them to participate in classes and/or regattas.

Prime inland waters with consistent wind are Lake Texoma, Canyon Lake, and Clear Lake. Corpus Christi and South Padre Island are considered premiere windsurfing locations. Windsurfers also give a nod of approval to Galveston Bay, North Padre Island, the Texas City Levee, Lake Ray Hubbard, Lake Travis, and Lake Texana. Beginners can also find lessons at Mud Lake/Lake Pasadena.

Corpus Christi Windsurfing Association
Sal Griffin
P.O. Box 87453
Corpus Christi, TX 78468
512-937-9521

Contact this address for specific information about windsurfing in the Corpus Christi area.

US SAILING
P.O. Box 209
Newport, RI 02840
401-849-5200
and
The Texas Sailing Association
David Greene
300 Rush Creek Dr. #A-6
Heath, TX 75087-8851
214-772-4880

This organization is a national governing body of competitive sailing. US SAILING is divided into councils that are further sub-divided into area Yacht Racing Associations. In Texas, the Yacht Racing Association is called the Texas Sailing Association. Becoming a member allows you to compete and participate in US SAILING regattas and attend special programs. The Youth division costs $12 to join and is open to anyone under 21.

US SAILING also can help if a child is interested in starting a sailing club or team in a local high school. The Interscholastic Sailing Organization is another helpful source for those wishing to set up junior programs in their community or school. For information, contact:

Interscholastic Sailing Organization (ISSA)
Larry White, President
P.O. Box 397
Niantic, CT 06357
201-739-3253

Junior Golden Anchor
Contact US SAILING

This program is available to any youth organization, school team or club, community sailing program, or junior yacht club group that signs up 100 percent of its members. The dues are $7.50, and coaches, parents, and community leaders can sign up for the adult Golden Anchor for $25. Members receive *American Sailor* magazine and helpful advice about running a sailing program.

Explorers

Along the Gulf Coast of Texas, Scout Explorer sailing and windsurfing posts are numerous. Check your local Boy Scout Council for ones in your area. This is a great opportunity to explore sailing or windsurfing with experienced leaders and without the high cost of equipment. For more information on Explorers, see page 60.

Start Sailing Right
United States Yacht Racing Union/American Red Cross
For Information about the program, contact:
USYRU—Training Office
Box 209
Newport, RI 02840
401-849-5200
or
American Red Cross
National Headquarters
17th and D Streets NW
Washington, DC 20006
202-737-8300

This combined effort by the country's governing racing body for sailing and the American Red Cross has produced a quality course for students wanting to learn to sail. The program consists of a pre-swim test and on-land and in-the-water instruction.

Learning to Sail Right uses the S.T.A.R. system, Standard for Training with Accelerated Results, which is a building-block approach with a lot of on-the-water practice.

The class is two-part and is open to children 10 years old and up. The first course is beginner and the second is advanced. The class culminates in both written and skills tests. Kids who pass earn a certificate.

An instruction book comes with the program and is recommended to be used in conjunction with *Learn to Sail* video tapes. The three-part tape for both the instructor and the student is available from the American Red Cross or the United States Yacht Racing Union.

Corpus Christi Sailing School [GC]
Corpus Christi Marina
P.O. Box 9277
Corpus Christi, TX 78401
512-882-7333

This city sailing program is a good example of how the Start Sailing Right Program can be implemented and can make sailing available to a wide group of children. Classes are offered each summer, starting at the end of May and running through the first of August. They are taught by Red Cross trained instructors in two-week-long sessions. Basic and intermediate classes are both available, with each lasting three hours a day. Kids ten years old and up learn how to rig a sunfish or dolphin, the basics of sailing, and eventually racing rules and strategies. Classes take place in the breakwater of the marina and on land. The cost is $70 per session.

Kids' Windsurfing & Kayak Lessons—Wind & Wave
    Watersports [GC]
10752 SPID
Corpus Christi, TX 78418
512-937-9283

This shop gives both windsurfing and kayak lessons on the shallow Laguna Madre, located on the way from Corpus Christi to Padre Island, locally called the "Mud Hole." Classes are held every day from April 1 to July 31. Kids age 6–18 take a three-hour lesson any time between 9:00 A.M. and 7:00 P.M. The cost is $45. Adults may also take classes. No experience in either sport is needed. For fun on your own, Wind & Wave also rents sailboards, kayaks, Boogie boards, and surfboards.

Wind & Wave offers group packages and tours for families, schools, and youth groups. Often they put groups in the water upwind of the landing site so they can paddle or sail easily back to land. Group tours can be arranged in other locations as well. One interesting and educational side trip is a paddle up the Oso Creek, which winds through the Corpus Christi Botanical Gardens.

Youth and Family Lessons—Texas Excursions [GC]
2705A Laguna Shores Road
Corpus Christi, TX 78418
512-937-2375

This business does it all! Master teachers Bob and Vicki Harraghy teach sailing, windsurfing, and kayaking to all ages and levels and specialize in beginners. Every month they sponsor a youth windsurfing clinic and offer group guided nature excursions on either sailboards or kayaks down the Laguna Madre. Rental equipment is also available.

Kids, and Group Lessons—WorldWinds Windsurfing [GC]
14225 SPID
Corpus Christi, TX 78418
512-949-7472
1-800-793-7471
Fax: 512-949-7436

WorldWinds is an authorized concessionaire of the National

Park Service located in the Padre Island National Seashore. WorldWinds gives lessons and provides rentals at Bird Island Basin, one of the best windsurfing locations in Texas. Bird Island Basin is part of the Laguna Madre, the body of water between Padre Island and the mainland. The first mile is shallow and the bottom is soft with sand and sea grass, which is ideal for beginners.

WorldWinds has special windsurfing equipment sized for children between 40 and 75 lbs. Private lessons for children are $30 for one hour and board and rig rentals are $10 an hour or $30 a day. Older children can join adults in up to three lessons for $45 each, which includes equipment. Private lessons are $30 an hour with your equipment or $25 an hour with rental equipment. Call for information on equipment rental only or on wetsuit rentals.

Chapter Five

✿

On Land Eco-Sports

When children participate in eco-sports, their playing field is Mother Earth: mountain-bike trails, rock faces, sandy beaches, and caves. Children not only have fun in these types of activities, they also learn respect for the land and our natural resources. These sports tend to be individual, challenging youngsters to better their own performances and skill level. However, most can be enjoyed with families and friends, in clubs, and in competitions. While the water sports in chapter 4 are also eco-sports, the ones in this chapter deal with activities on land. For other opportunities, check the day camps and programs listed in chapter 2 and the overnight camps in chapter 8.

Texas Wildlife Expo
Expo Coordinator, TPWD
4200 Smith School Road
Austin, TX 78744
1-800-792-1112
512-389-4472

This annual exposition typically takes place at the end of September or beginning of October at the Parks & Recreation

Wildlife Department headquarters in Austin. It is sponsored by Texas Parks & Wildlife and various corporate sponsors as a means for people to pass on the outdoor tradition to their families and friends. In past years, about half of those attending were children, and it's no wonder. There is plenty for children to see and do at this recreational and educational event. Visitors can watch demonstrations and view displays related to hunting, camping, fishing, and outdoor fun. Probably the biggest draw, though, are the hands-on activities. Kids can shoot a bow and arrow, fire a shot gun, catch a fish, or scale a climbing wall. Newer events include the 90-foot-by-120-foot "wet zone," a manmade waterway where children can learn and practice canoeing and water safety, and a Wilderness Challenge orienteering course.

Rock Climbing

Most instructors agree that children, even very young ones, are naturals at this sport. They are agile, lightweight, and have a nice balance between arm and leg motion. Of course, not every child has easy access to rock faces that are appropriate for climbing. Luckily, indoor gyms, conveniently located in urban areas, offer a safe supervised alternative for children to learn and practice climbing. Indoor gyms also give families planning an outdoor climbing trip a chance to learn the sport before they go.

Rock climbing involves three basic methods: bouldering, top roping, and lead climbing. *Bouldering* is climbing sideways or horizontally on large boulder-like stone faces and is good training that can be practiced inside and used outdoors. It forces kids to use their minds to plan where they will move next. Most gyms that offer indoor climbing have pitches and inclines to make bouldering in certain areas more difficult.

Top-roping is done inside since it requires a set fulcrum from which to hang a rope above the climber and two people below to act as belays. Since there is no fulcrum outside set in the rocks, when climbing outdoors climbers must create their own fulcrum using bolts, rock clips (called quick draws), and their rope. This method is called *lead climbing* and is the primary method used to climb outdoors. Lead climbing can be safely practiced inside as well. Some outdoor areas prohibit bolts, and so experienced climbers must use a fourth technique called *Pro*, which stands for passive and active resistance. This is very difficult, requiring the climber to thread wire shrouds through crevices of rocks to create a fulcrum.

Indoor and Outdoor Rock Climbing Opportunities

Austin Nature Center Climbing for Kids
301 Nature Center Drive
Austin, TX 78746
512-327-8181

Throughout the year, the Austin Nature Center takes kids 10 through 15 on a rock-climbing adventure at Reimer Ranch. The day starts with basic lessons about equipment, techniques, and safety. Then the group goes to try its skills. No equipment is necessary, but climbers should wear either climbing shoes or closed-toed shoes. Kids can rent shoes as well. Participants should also bring a lunch, a water bottle, and snacks.

The center takes a minimum of 6 kids and a maximum of 12. The fee for the clinic is $40, and it runs from 8:00 A.M. until 4:00 P.M.

Biron Gymnastics [GC]
1322 S. Dairy
Ashford, TX 77077
713-497-6666

This gymnastics school has a special "Rock and Roll" class for children ages 7 and up. Children learn all about rock climbing, including knot-tying, safety, identifying and using equipment, and climbing techniques. Older kids, 12 and up, learn to belay as well. Classes run $70 for four sessions. Experienced climbers can also drop in and participate in an open climb, which typically costs $6. Groups are welcome if they make prior arrangements.

This gym has also recently initiated ropes courses for both adults and children. This is a group activity which includes both high and low elements that challenge children in a safe, regulated setting. The ropes course costs $15 for a 3-hour session. Call in advance to schedule and register a class.

Enchanted Rock State Natural Area
Route 4, Box 17
Fredricksburg, TX 78624
915-247-3903

Not far from San Antonio and only 18 miles from Fredricksburg, this site is a great rock-climbing location. The Indians are said to have feared the large granite rocks there because they believed the glistening moonlight on the rocks was ghost fires. The rock is formed in a large dome approximately 640 acres large and 500 feet high. The park is open year-round but is subject to closure during peak periods, when a maximum number of visitors enter. The site is so popular that, unfortunately, it has experienced problems with erosion and tree loss due to so many feet passing through it.

Exposure Indoor Rock Climbing
6970-C FM 1960 West
Houston, TX 77069
713-397-9446

Most of Exposure's customers are children, particularly Cub Scouts, church groups, youth groups, and parties. There is no minimum age, but kids 17 and under are required to have a parent sign a liability form. In addition, roping belayers must be at least 12 years old.

The manager suggests that groups make reservations a month in advance, but they will fit in groups any time if possible. An all-day pass costs $8 and rental of all gear is $6. Exposure offers a group discount. Its hours are 1:00 P.M. to 10:00 P.M. Monday through Thursday, 1:00 P.M. to 11:00 P.M. Friday, 10:00 A.M. to 11:00 P.M. Saturday, and 11:00 A.M. to 8:00 P.M. Sunday.

Hueco Tanks State Park [BB]
Rural Route 3, Box 1
El Paso, TX 79935
915-857-1135

Located 26 miles east of El Paso, this park got its name from the natural rock basins or "huecos" in the rocks that trap water from infrequent rains. The rocks are also the canvas of ancient Native American pictographs, and there has been some vandalism and graffiti in the past, but not likely by the climbers. On busy days, the Tanks are the playground to more than 400 climbers, both professional and amateur, from all over the United States. The park campground is usually booked solid from November to February, when the weather is cool. To control a continually growing crowd, rangers have begun to limit the number of visitors into the park. Only 125 vehicles are allowed in per day, and the gate is locked from sunset to 8:00 A.M. Call ahead to make camp reservations.

Lake Mineral Wells State Park [PL]
Superintendent
Rt. 4, Box 39C
Mineral Wells, TX 76067
817-328-1171

This state park is located on over 2,800 acres of post-oak woodlands and meadows. Climbers like the variety of rock formations mixed with trees and greenery. The park also features a 673-acre lake, hiking trails, extensive day-use facilities, and overnight facilities.

Outpost Wilderness Adventure
P.O. Box 511
Hunt, TX 78024
830-238-4383 or 830-238-4650
e-mail: hoh@owa.com
Contact: David Appleton

Outpost Wilderness Adventure is a guided outdoor adventure company that offers clinics on weekends through the winter that focus on rock climbing. These are held at state parks, including Enchanted Rock, Lake Mineral Wells, and Hueco Tanks. The clinics are open to children and, in fact, kids often make up the majority of students participating. Call for a current schedule and prices. Learn more about Outpost Wilderness Adventure camp in chapter 8.

Pseudo Rock [HC]
200 Trinity
Austin, TX 78701
512-474-4376

This 10,000 square foot indoor climbing gym offers classes for all ages, including children. There is no minimum age, but children under 16 must be accompanied by a parent. The facility is open to groups as well.

Pseudo Rock also takes climbers to Enchanted Rock State Park and Hueco Tanks State Park to learn to climb outdoors. Families with children and youth groups are welcome. Pseudo Rock provides all the equipment and transportation. The cost is $60 per person, per day. Group rates are sometimes available. Call for reservations and a class schedule.

Spelunking

Kids who don't suffer from claustrophobia may want to try spelunking, the amateur pursuit of cave exploration and study. Both adults and children can enjoy spelunking as either a relaxed afternoon side trip or a serious hobby, and kids who live in areas with caves may find a grotto, or a caving club they can join. This can be a dirty pursuit, so dress kids appropriately and remember to wear something warm, since caves can be chilly. Kids should wear gripping shoes, carry three sources of light, and never go caving alone.

Austin Nature Center, After School Caving [HC]
301 Nature Center Drive
Austin, TX 78746
512-327-8181

Children ages 7 through 12 who live in the Austin area can meet at the nature center to learn all about how caves are formed and what lives inside them. The group then goes spelunking in a local cave. The center provides all equipment. Students need to wear long pants and long-sleeved shirts that they can get dirty. Bring a flashlight, a snack, and a water bottle. The class runs from 4:00 to 7:30 P.M. Call for an exact date. The cost for the class is $18.

Gorman Cave—Colorado Bend State Park [HC]
10 miles south of Bend on County Road 792
915-628-3240

On weekends, take a family or group on one of the tours through Gorman Caves located on this 5,328-acre state park on the Colorado River. The walking tour starts at 9:15 on Saturday and Sunday and leads you through Gorman Cave. The fee is $10 per person. A more difficult tour of progressively smaller caves begins at 1:30 on Saturdays and costs $15 per person. The park also offers walking tours around Gorman Falls. Children 5 and under tour free and kids ages 6 to 12 years old pay $1. Older kids and adults pay $2. The park is open 24 hours a day, with an entrance fee of $2 per person, $7 to camp. Reservations are required.

Kickapoo Cavern State Natural Area [HC]
40 miles west of Uvalde on Ranch Rd. 674
210-563-2342

Grab a flashlight and take this special tour of Kickapoo Cavern. In May, rangers lead a group tour of this undeveloped cave. The tour runs from 4:00 until 6:00 P.M. Children 12 and under pay $2. Teens and adults pay $5. Reservations and TCP membership are required for this tour.

Orienteering

Orienteering has been called "jogging for thinkers," since participants must not only run, they must use a compass and map to guide them through a course with a series of checkpoints. High schools and sometimes middle schools have orienteering clubs, and they are a good place to start for older kids, but children of all ages can participate to some degree in orienteering. Adult competitions often include a special children's course called string orienteering.

String orienteering implements a short route in which children can hold the strings to follow the course. Like older children and adults, they must stop at check points and have their card stamped. This familiarizes younger children with the routine and feel of orienteering. The only items of equipment kids need to start orienteering are a compass and hiking boots. Two active groups in Texas can guide you to the nearest orienteering competition:

Houston Orienteering Club
P.O. Box 18251
Houston, TX 77023
North Texas Orienteering Association
P.O. Box 832464
Richardson, TX 75083

US Orienteering Foundation
P.O. Box 1444
Forest Park, GA 30051

Contact this organization to start an orienteering club in a school or to find out more about the sport and setting up competitions.

Dallas Nature Center [PL]
7171 Mountain Creek Parkway
Dallas, TX 75249
214-296-1955

Try your hand at orienteering at the Dallas Nature Center. The center offers group orienteering for all ages. Kids will use compasses to navigate through various courses at the center. Call to set up a time for your group or class. For more information on the center, see chapter 2, pags 16–18.

Texoma Lutheran Camp [PL]
Route 1, Box 116-P
Potsboro, TX 75076
903-786-3121
888-886-6198
e-mail: lomtexoma@texoma.net
Director—Keith Lund

Each year, on the second weekend in November, Texoma
Lutheran Camp hosts the Texoma Orienteering Meet. This 2-day
competition is open to individuals, families, and school, youth,
and church groups across Texas. Each year, over 600 people par-

ticipate, about two-thirds of them children. On Saturday morning, the camp directs orienteering clinics and then the race is on. Competition continues on Sunday, and there is a special night-orienteering session for fun on Sunday. Participants stay on the premises and at local motels in the area. For more on this camp and its summer program, see chapter 8.

Mountain Biking and Hiking

Hikers can enjoy more than one thousand miles of nature trails in Texas. Many of these trails can be used for mountain biking and horse riding as well. A good portion of these areas are in state parks, and TPW can send you a brochure called *Mountain Biking State Parks,* an excellent listing of state parks that allow mountain biking. The brochure lists the total miles of trails available at each park and their difficulty level, as well as other facilities at the park, such as tent camping and backpacking trails. A good book which describes and analyzes the hiking trails in Texas is *Hiking and Backpacking Trails of Texas* by Mickey Little .

Mountain Biking

Children typically get involved in mountain or off-road biking because their parents participate in the sport. However, youngsters can get information about biking opportunities by contacting a bicycle shop in their town or by linking up with a bike club. Some high schools may also sponsor off-road bicycling clubs.

Texas Bicycle Coalition
P.O. Box 1121
Austin, TX 78767
512-476-RIDE
http:\\www.ccsi.com\~tbca

Children may participate as a beginner or in a higher class in series and non-series races in Texas. The Texas Bicycle Coalition can help you find out about upcoming races. Call, or better yet, visit their website to find out about off-road opportunities with the Texas Off-road Mountain Biking Association.

Bluff Creek Ranch
Paul Nolan
Warda, TX 78960
409-242-5894

In the fall, this ranch hosts the Geberstage Gallop, which includes the national finals of the American Mountain Bike Challenge and the International Mountain Biking finals of the Pan American Games. The National Off-road Bicycle Riders Association sponsors both. Children 12 and under can enter free. Older children and adults pay $5 for riding only and $7 for riding and overnight camping.

State Parks

State Parks are a wonderful place to both mountain-bike and hike, and most have well-established trails. Popular parks with easy mountain-biking trails for children and beginners include:

Kerrville-Schreiner State Park [HC]
210-257-5392
Located on the southern edge of Kerrville on Texas 173.

Pedernales Falls State Park [HC]
210-868-7304
Located eight miles east of Johnson City on FM 2766.

McKinney Falls State [HC]
512-243-1643
Located thirteen miles from downtown Austin. Take U.S. 183 south to the scenic Loop Rd., then go west to the park entrance.

Lake Somerville State Park [PL]
409-535-7763
North of Brenham off State Highway 36

Mountain Bike Trail Ride—San Angelo State Park [PP]
915-949-4757 or 915-947-2687
North entrance—take US 87 to FM 2288. South entrance—take US 67 to FM 2288

In April, ride along more than 20 miles of riding trails with other mountain bikers. The event begins at 10:00 A.M. and ends at 1:00 P.M. Reservations are required. Admission is $2 for adults and $1 for kids under 17. TCP members participate free.

Hiking

Dallas Nature Center—10-K Walks
7171 Mountain Creek Parkway
Dallas, TX 75249
214-296-1955
or
The Dallas Trekkers
c/o Bruce Fitch
2120 Statler Dr.
Carrollton, TX 75007
972-323-9977

These two 10-K walks at the Dallas Nature Center are sponsored by the Dallas Trekkers and sanctioned by the American Volkssport Association and the International Volkssport Verband. This means walkers can earn credit toward IVV Achievement Awards. All age walkers are welcome in this event; however, children under 12 must be accompanied by an adult. All participants must carry a start card. Awards are given to the first 75 people to walk.

The walk is held in May and walkers should pre-register. There is a small fee for walking and a $3 fee per vehicle. Trail maps cost 25 cents.

Friedrich Park [HC]
21395 Milsa Road
San Antonio, TX 78256
210-698-1057

Located in the northwest area of San Antonio, this park consists of 230 acres of natural wildlife and plant life. The park offers eight hiking trails that vary in difficulty and distance, three-quarters of a mile of hard surface trail, and 3.6 miles of natural surface. The Forest Range Trail is near the entrance and is an easy start. It takes about thirty minutes to walk, has hand ropes, and is handicapped accessible. Other trails are more challenging, such as the Main Loop, which connects and branches off to other trails.

The park is open Wednesdays through Saturdays, 8:00 A.M. to 8:00 P.M., April through September, and 8:00 A.M. to 5:00 P.M., October through March.

Lone Star Hiking Trail—Sam Houston National Forest [PW]
San Jacinto District
308 North Belcher (FM 2025)
Cleveland, TX 77327

409-6462 or 6463
Raven District
P.O. Drawer 1000
(FM 1375)
New Waverly, TX 77358
409-344-6205

The Lone Star Hiking Trail began in 1968 with the help of a small group of Houston Sierra Club members. With the assistance of the US Forestry Service, they laid out a trail in the Sam Houston National Forest. Other groups got involved, including the Boy Scouts, the Girl Scouts, the Youth Conservation Corps, and the Sierra Club. Today the trail reaches about 140 miles and is maintained primarily by the Forest Service.

For specific regulations about hiking and camping along the Lone Star Trail or to purchase maps, contact:

Forest Supervisor
701 North First Street
Lufkin, TX 75901

Texas Forestry Association's Woodland Trails [PW]
Box 1488
Lufkin, TX 75902-1288
409-632-TREE

The Texas Woodland Trails is a series of 11 hiking paths in east Texas. These were chosen by the Texas Forestry Association, one of the oldest conservation organizations in the state. Many of the trails are wheelchair accessible. Youth groups that hike six of the trails receive a special patch as a reward. Those who walk all 11 paths receive an additional red star. An adult leader must validate the accomplishment. This program is approved by the Girl Scouts and the Boy Scouts.

Sandy Adventures

Kids naturally take to the sand. Release them at the beach, and they instantly run to the dunes to slide, roll, and jump. They can spend hours burying each other in wet sand or building sandcastles and other creations. These sandy adventures are sure to capture children's imagination and energy.

Sons of the Beach with the Amazing Walter and
    Sandy Feet [GC]
On the beach behind the hotels
South Padre Island Chamber of Commerce
1-800-SO-PADRE or 210-761-6433

For a special treat, watch these two pros construct art from sand on the beach at South Padre Island. If kids want to learn all the tricks of the trade, they can take a lesson from the duo for $25. Times and days are based on appointments.

South Padre Island Sandcastle Days [GC]
Contact: Iris Hernandez, SPI CVB
210-761-9462 or 1-800-SO-PADRE
e-mail: sandyfeet@main.rgv.net

For fun in the sun and creative nature art, try this annual sandcastle-building event held in mid-October at Bahia Mar Resort on South Padre Island. In addition to the masters division, the competition features an amateur division for elementary kids' groups, secondary age children either in groups or as individuals, families, and adults. Cash prizes are awarded for the first three places, and there is no entry fee or pre-registration.

This is a two-division event, one for amateurs and another for professionals. Five to ten sandcastle professionals join in and compete along with the amateurs. They spend up to 16 hours building artistic structures of every imaginable subject. Once you finish your sandcastle, sit back and enjoy watching the pros. Some of the structures are huge and sure to impress young sculptors and spectators.

Sand Surfing—Monahans Sandhills State Park [BB]
P.O. Box 1738
Monahans, TX 79756
1-800-792-1112
Rates & Reservations: 1-512-389-8900

If your kids are landlubbers instead of water people, try sand surfing at Monahans Sandhills instead of at the beach. This unique park is located six miles northeast of Monahans off I-20 on Park Road 41, less than an hour's drive west of Midland. So what is Monahans? Try 3,840 acres of sand dunes—some as much as 70 feet high.

Kids can rent boards and disks at the concession building to "surf" down the shiny sand hills. When the weather heats up, escape to the shade shelters for a break, get a soft drink, or enjoy the interpretive center.

Chapter Six

Birding & Nature Watching

Nature tourism is the fastest growing segment of the travel industry in the United States. Birding as a sport, for example, has reached new heights, with an estimated 61 million birders across the country. Texas, with its abundance of wildlife and vast array of resident and migratory birds, is a natural destination for those who love to observe and photograph wildlife. Texas has close to 600 documented bird species, many of which are found in no other state.

Birding, nature watching, and outdoor photography are activities children and families can enjoy almost anywhere, from outings in the backyard to camping trips in state or national parks.

Birding

The Great Texas Birding Trail
Texas Parks & Wildlife: 1-800-792-1112
Texas Department of Highways: 1-800-452-9292
Audubon Statewide Rare Bird Alert: 713-992-2757

The Gulf Coast and Rio Grande Valley are home to over 400 species of birds, including resident and migratory birds. In order to help travelers and birders make the most of viewing our feathered friends, the state of Texas created The Great Texas Coastal Birding Trail along the Gulf Coast. The route runs the length of the coast, with marked stops and observation areas along the way. In addition, there are loops that take visitors off the main route to specific birding areas. The Trail is divided into three sections: Upper, Central, and Lower Texas Coast. Call to receive a full-color map of each section with marked stops, detailed descriptions, and directions.

Great Texas Birding Classic [GC]
Texas Parks & Wildlife Department
4200 Smith School Rd.
Austin, TX 78744
512-389-4800 or
1-800-TX-BIRDS

This is the granddaddy of birding events and in fact is billed as "the biggest, longest and wildest birding competition ever held in the United States." For a full week in April, birders along the Texas Gulf Coast compete to spot the hundreds of birds commonly found along The Great Texas Coastal Birding Trail. In communities along the coast, there are special events, children's activities, poster contests, and art auctions in conjunction with the competition.

The Great Texas Birding Classic has a special division just for students. There are two divisions: the Youth Division, for kids in grades 6 through 12, and the College Teams Division, for students currently attending a college or university. Teams of three to six members compete in one of three regions on any of the official birding days. For the registration fees, students receive literature, T-shirts, Birding Trail maps, and tickets to the awards brunch. The TPW seeks sponsors to pay for the costs of competitors, or students may collect pledges for each bird sighted.

Texas Birding Festivals

Birding festivals are a fun way to learn about a particular species of bird indigenous to an area of the state. Along with displays, printed information, watching opportunities, and seminars, the festivals below offer specific activities to spur young people's interest in birds and birding.

EagleFest (January) [PL]
P.O. Box 695
Emory, TX 75440
903-473-2377

Located outside of Dallas on Lakes Fork and Tawakoni, this festival celebrates the approximately 60 bald eagles that winter here. Take an eagle tour by barge or watch live demonstrations with birds of prey.

CraneFest (February) [PP]
Big Spring Chamber of Commerce/Convention and
    Visitors' Bureau
P.O. Box 1391
Big Spring, TX 79721
915-263-7641

Tour the Comanche Trail Park and Scenic Mountain State Park and observe Sandhill Cranes, waterfowl, and more than 60 other species of wintering birds. The festival also offers live presentations with birds, native plant study, and historic rock carvings.

Whooping Crane Winter Bird Festival (February) [GC]
Rockport/Fulton Area Chamber of Commerce
404 Broadway
Rockport, TX 78382
1-800-242-0071

Observe more than 500 species in this area of Texas, including the only remaining wild whooping cranes. Tours of the Aransas National Wildlife Refuge are also offered.

Attwater's Prairie Chicken Festival (March) [PL]
Eagle Lake Chamber of Commerce
408 E. Main St.
Eagle Lake, TX 77434-2534
409-234-2780

Celebrate these odd-looking endangered birds at Eagle Lake next to the Attwater's Prairie Chicken National Wildlife Refuge. Along with wildlife tours and presentations, children will appreciate the wonderful display of wildflowers.

Hummer Bird Celebration (September) [GC]
Rockport, TX
512-729-6445 or 1-800-826-6441

Join in a fun coastal festival each September that celebrates the hummingbirds that make a stop in the Rockport-Fulton area on their migration to Mexico. Families can take birdwatching trips and purchase hummingbird-related items at booths. They'll also learn about outdoor and nature photography and how to attract hummingbirds in their own backyard. There are special birding games and projects for the kids, along with demonstrations by the rescue and rehabilitation group called Last Chance Forever.

Annual Bluebird Festival (April) [PL]
Wills Point Chamber of Commerce
P.O. Box 217
Wills Point, TX 75169
903-873-3111

You'll likely see more Eastern Bluebirds here than anywhere else in Texas along with nesting boxes, arts, crafts, and educational displays.

Migration Celebration (April) [GC]
Southern Brazoria County Visitor Bureau
420 Hwy. 332
Cleut, TX 77531
1-800-938-4853

Watch the migratory birds fill the sky as they return to their Texas coast wintering grounds. Workshops and tours are available at Brazoria, San Bernard, and the Big Boggy National Wildlife Refuges. Kids may spot many of the 350 species of birds in this area.

Bats

Bats are not the dreadful, blood-sucking beasts of horror movies. They don't suck blood or attack your hair, but are really helpful since they eat hundreds of insects, including mosquitoes. Texas is home to 32 of the 42 bat species found in the United States. For easy viewing, try catching the bats under the Congress

Avenue Bridge in Austin, home to one million bats. For other viewing spots and organized trips that will make kids batty, try these four state parks:

Devil's Sinkhole State Natural Area [HC]
135 miles northwest of San Antonio in Edwards County
210-563-2342

During various times of the year, park manager and biologist D. Stuart leads groups to the sinkhole to observe the bats. The sinkhole is the result of a collapsed cave that left a vertical orb in the rocks. It is about 150 feet deep and so is not open to the general public except on the tour. The freetail bats fly up and out of the hole in a counterclockwise vortex. The tour starts at 6:00 P.M., and for children under 12, the admission fee is $5. Older kids and adults pay $8 and TCP members pay $6. Reservations are required.

Fort Leaton State Historical Site
P.O. Box 1220
Presidio, TX 79845
915-229-3613

Some 30,000 bats migrate to this area each spring from the wintering grounds in Mexico. Unfortunately they were making their home in the ceiling of the historical fort. The management built a 12-foot-by-12-foot bat house using similar materials as were used in the fort in hopes the bats would transfer to their new home. While some of the bats still prefer "hanging out" in the fort, many have successfully transfered to their new home. Visiters may view them in and around both buildings. Admission to Fort Leaton is $2.50 per person.

Kickapoo Cavern State Natural Area [BB]
40 miles west of Uvalde on Ranch Rd. 674
210-563-2342

Children will be delighted when they witness the evening emergence of the Brazilian freetail bats. The Green Cave in this area is said to be the home of two million bats. The tour starts at 6:00 P.M. The fee is $2 per child under 12 and $5 for older children and adults. A TCP member must accompany each vehicle to take this tour.

The Old Tunnel Wildlife Management Area
Blanco State Park
210-833-4333

Two million Mexican freetail bats live in the management area from March to October. Arrive one hour before sunset, and you can often see them emerge from the old 920-foot-long tunnel. Visitors should watch for the bats from either the deck or the trail, since the park does not allow anyone in the tunnel or near the entrance.

TCP tours are conducted on Thursday and Saturday evenings from June to October.

Dolphin Watching

Bottle-nosed dolphins are beautiful and fascinating creatures to watch. They are naturally friendly and often swim beside boats in the Gulf of Mexico and bay waters up and down the coast. The following programs will take families and youth groups to see the dolphins in the wild.

Dolphin I. [GC]
Hospitality Docks next to Queen Isabella Causeway
Port Isabel
210-943-1621

Watch the playful antics of the local dolphins on this 42-foot boat with indoor and outdoor seating and netted safety rails. Capt. Joey Adair gives a narration and doles out trivia about the animals, calling them by name. Two-hour trips depart daily at 10:00 A.M. and 5:30 P.M. The fare is $10 for children, with no charge for those under 2. Adults pay $15, and seniors receive a $3 discount. Ask about private charters and discounts for school and youth groups.

Dolphin Watch [GC]
Route1, Box 297-A
Ingleside, TX 78362
512-776-2887

This trip into Corpus Christi Bay is open daily year-round, weather permitting, and lasts about one hour. The guides are very familiar with over sixty local dolphins. They can tell them apart and have even given them names. The tour boat can take 6–12 people at a time, and can accommodate youth groups and classes in back-to-back shifts. The trip costs $12 for youngsters age 12 and under and $17 for teens and adults. Call to make reservations and get directions.

Dolphin Watch Nature Tours aboard the *Duke* [GC]
Woody's Sport Center
Port Aransas, TX 78373
512-749-6969

The *Duke* takes a sunset cruise to spot dolphins at play. In addition, its crew pulls a plankton net and lets passengers view the catch through a discovery scope. The captain points out shorebirds such as bright pink rosette spoonbills and tall, stately herons. Finally, the crew pulls a shrimp trawl net and dumps out the catch for a quick observation of the wide variety of fish, shrimp, and other marine life in the water.

Texas Wildflowers

Texans look forward to spring wildflowers with the same zeal with which folks from other states look forward to fall leaves turning colors. On years with abundant rainfall, the flowers can blanket roadsides and fields. While Texas boasts more than 5,000 species of flowering plants, the bluebonnet, which is the state flower, probably gets the most attention. Families often use the colorful spring wildflowers as a photo backdrop.

The National Wildflower Research Center
4801 La Crosse Blvd.
Austin, TX 78739
512-292-4100

The National Wildflower Research Center is Lady Bird Johnson's brainchild. The goal of the center is to preserve, protect, and promote the use of wildflowers and other native plants. The center has displays of native plants and flowers, formal gardens such as the butterfly and hummingbird gardens, and gardens for the visually impaired, planted with aromatic plants. The center propagates over 500 species of native wildflowers. Children will delight in the Children's Little House, with a four-foot-high door. The center also offers a Children's Nature Discovery program to teach children about the importance of native flora.

The center is open Tuesday through Sunday from 9:00 A.M. until 5:30 P.M. Admission is free to members (membership costs $25). Students pay $2 and those 18 months old to 5 years pay $1. Adult nonmembers pay $3.50. Guided tours are available to groups. Call for reservations.

Wildflower Hotlines

Call the following hotlines in the area you live in or are visiting to find out the peak time to view wildflowers.

The Texas Department of Transportation—800-452-9292
The National Wildflower Research Center—
    512-292-4100 (Mid-March through May)
East Texas Tourism Wildflower Hot Line—903-757-4444
Lake Buchanan Hot Line—512-793-2803
South Texas Wildflower Line—512-886-4848, ext. 1053

Wildflower Tour in Cleburne State Park
Rt. 2, Box 90
Cleburne, TX 76031
817-645-4215

Kids will love this tour. Not only will they get to see fields of colorful flowers, they also get to tour the park on a hayride. The ranger guides two tours in late April, each lasting an hour and a half. One starts at 10:00 A.M. and the other at 2:00 P.M. The fee is $3 per family.

The DeWitt County Wildflower Association [SP]
312 E. Broadway
Cuero, TX 77954
512-275-9942

During the annual "Dewitt County Lanes and Byways" celebration, this association offers three-hour guided tours of lush fields of flowers. The celebration is held each April and includes a bike tour and a special Walk Thru the Flowers program. The association is open to groups and will work with area school districts to coordinate wildflower information for science and art projects.

State Parks & Wildlife Management Areas

State parks are a good place to watch wildlife whether you're driving, hiking, or just sitting under a tree. Each offers a unique experience, and many provide special tours and classes for families or children. A good way to keep track of events in various parks is to check the calendar in the monthly *Texas Parks & Wildlife* magazine or purchase a Texas Conservation Passport to receive the *Texas Conservation Passport Journal.* For more information on passports, see chapter 1, page 4.

Texas Wildlife Management Areas are a wonderful way to educate children by exposing them to more undeveloped areas of the state. These areas may not include as many facilities as state parks, but they often have research programs and demonstrations that visitors may observe. Always call in advance when you plan to visit one to make certain you can gain access. The best time to catch the biologist in the office is on weekdays from 8:00 to 9:00 A.M. and 12:00 to 1:00 P.M.

Barton Warnock Environmental Education Center [BB]
HC 70, Box 375
Terlingua, TX 79852
915-424-3327

This center serves as one of the entry points into Big Bend State Natural Area. It's housed in a Spanish-style building with exhibits on the archeology, geology, wildlife, and history of the area. The four-acre Desert Garden is a wonderful place to view plants and cacti native to the Chihuahuan Desert.

Dinosaur Valley State Park [HC]
P.O. Box 396
Glen Rose, TX 76043
817-897-4588

For a look at life in Texas before humans made their mark, kids will enjoy searching for giant dinosaur tracks in Dinosaur Valley State Park. There are tracks of three types of dinosaurs dating back about 105 million years. Take the 1-mile hiking trail that crosses the Paluxy River and presents a sweeping view of the park, or the Cedar Brake Trail with alternate trails and five scenic overlooks.

U.S. Fish and Wildlife Refuges and Hatcheries

The first national wildlife refuge was established in 1903 by President Theodore Roosevelt in order to protect Florida's egrets, herons, and other birds from hunters who were killing them for their feathers. Since that time, the need to protect animals and their habitats has grown as industrial development and population have increased. Texas is part of the Southwest Region, which includes 2,400,000 acres of land in four states.

There are currently fifteen refuges and three hatcheries in the state with diverse wildlife to observe, including many endangered species, such as the Attwater's prairie chicken and the black-capped vireo. Some refuges do not allow visitors, and others may have restricted areas to protect nesting grounds, so call ahead for more information. Many offer special tours, educational programs, and nature trails. Write for a complete directory and colorful map of the refuges in the Southwest Region.

U.S. Fish and Wildlife Refuges and Hatcheries
  (Southwest Region)
P.O. Box 1306
Albuquerque, NM 87103-1306
505-766-3940
Texas—1-800-735-2988

Anahuac National Wildlife Refuge [PW]
P.O. Box 278
Anahuac, TX 77514
409-267-3337 or 409-839-2680

Anahuac is "The Gator Capital of Texas," because alligators outnumber the people. You can view them along with a wealth of other wildlife, including waterfowl and neotropical migrant song-birds, on this 30,000-acre reserve. The refuge is home to over 75,000 migrating snow geese and 22 species of ducks. Also expect to see great blue herons, roseate spoonbills, shrimp, crabs, snakes, and turtles. There is a 12-mile-long road through the refuge but there are no hiking trails.

Aransas National Wildlife Refuge Complex [GC]
P.O. Box 100
Austwell, TX 77950
512-286-3559

This refuge and the surrounding area are famous as the wintering grounds for the endangered whooping crane. Visitors can reach the 113,000-acre refuge by car or boat. There is a paved 15-mile auto loop drive from the Wildlife Interpretive Center to the Observation Tower and back. All visitors must check in at the Interpretive Center each day they visit. Admission is $2 per car.

Several tour boats out of the Rockport/Fulton area specialize in ferrying visitors over to bird watch and most offer educational narration, restrooms, beverages, and bird checklists. Once at the refuge, visitors can hike or bike and observe and photograph the cranes, as well as more than 389 species of other birds. The refuge is also home to feral hogs, deer, javelinas, armadillos, cougars, bobcats, and alligators.

The refuge is open from sunrise to sunset daily and the center is open from 7:30 A.M. to 5:00 P.M. Groups can reserve a time to watch films or listen to lectures. Overnight facilities are available to school and youth groups that call ahead to make plans; however, there is no other general camping.

Attwater's Prairie Chicken National Wildlife Refuge [PL]
P.O. Box 519
Eagle Lake, TX 77434
409-234-3021

The primary purpose of this 8,000-acre refuge is to protect the habitat of the endangered Attwater's prairie chicken. The refuge has two hiking trails and an auto tour route. Visitors may photograph and view the prairie birds, neotropicals, and various reptiles, mammals, and amphibians. Check first, however, since the prairie chickens are very protected, and you may be restricted or banned from viewing their habitat.

Laguna Atascosa National Wildlife Refuge [GC]
P.O. Box 450
Rio Hondo, TX 78583-0450
210-748-3607

This refuge located in the Rio Grande Valley is a premier bird-watching location. There are 393 species of birds here, including seven that are endangered. Eighty percent of the North American population of redhead ducks winter here, and Laguna Atascosa is also home to two endangered cats. The refuge has hiking trails and auto tours, a visitor center, and educational programs.

Other Great Viewing Opportunities

Cockrell Butterfly Center [GC]
1 Hermann Circle Drive at the Museum of Natural Science in
    Hermann Park
Houston, TX
713-639-4600
713-639-4629 (in Spanish: 713-639-4603)

This fascinating exhibit is dedicated to showcasing butterflies. Kids can totally surround themselves with thousands of these beautiful creatures in a rainforest setting. Enter from an underground cave behind a 40-foot waterfall and emerge among queen palms and papayas plants with recorded rainforest sounds playing in the background. Children can even watch the butterflies hatching in viewing boxes.

Visit the Brown Hall of Entomology to see several thousand butterflies, moths, and beetles and learn about their lives and place in nature. The center is located in the Houston Museum of Natural Science in Hermann Park (see chapter 2, page 19). It is open Monday through Saturday from 9:00 A.M. to 6:00 P.M., and Sundays from noon to 6:00 P.M. Children under 12 pay only $2 for admittance, and older kids and adults pay $3. There is a discount for groups of 20 or more. School groups making advance reservations are charged $1 per person.

Fennessey Ranch [GC]
P.O. Box 99
Bayside, TX 78340
512-529-6600

The Fennessey Ranch is a privately owned nature preserve now open to the public for the first time in its 161-year history. The several-thousand-acre preserve includes wetlands, lakes, meadows, woodlands, rivers, and uplands. Kids may spot one of more than 400 species of birds and 50 kinds of amphibians and reptiles.

Fennessey runs tours on Thursdays and Saturdays starting at 8:00 A.M. and lasting approximately 3½ hours. While families can sign up for a group tour with other visitors, the ranch also offers special tours for school groups, 4-H Clubs, and other youth associations. These tours tend to move quicker and information and methods are geared to the particular group's age and interests. A tour for young children might include identifying two birds, three trees, two bird calls, and two reptiles, for example. Tours also include a hayride, hiking, birding, plant study, tracking, and history study of the area. Reservations are required and gates are kept locked. Admission for tours is $15 per person, with discounts for groups.

Fort Worth Nature Center and Refuge [PL]
Texas 199
Fort Worth, TX
817-237-1111

This refuge began as Greer Island Nature Center and has grown to 3,500 acres of nature trails and wildlife. Children might see roaming bison and deer among the plants. The center has an interpretive center, hiking, and self-guiding information for hiking. The center is open Tuesday through Saturday from 9:00 A.M. to 5:00 P.M., and from noon to 4:30 P.M. on Sunday.

Galveston Lab [GC]
National Marine Fisheries
Avenue U at 50th Street
Galveston, TX 77554
409-766-3670

Come see as many as 600 sea turtles at this marine fisheries facility. Among the species reared and studied here are the Kemp's Ridley and Loggerhead turtles of all ages and sizes. The animals are kept in tanks, and anyone is welcome to observe them on Tuesdays, Thursdays, and Saturdays at 10:00 and 11:00 A.M. and 1:00 and 2:00 P.M. School and youth groups should call ahead of time. The tour is free.

The Texas Zoo [SP]
P.O. Box 69
Victoria, TX 77902
512-573-7681

This small zoo located on 7 acres in Riverside Park is the only zoo in the nation devoted entirely to showing and tending animals native to one particular state. The animals represent the ten different habitats that exist in Texas and include such species as ocelots, red foxes, deer, snakes, spiders, and a buzzard named "Yacky."

Some animals represented at the zoo are not so plentiful in the state nowadays, including a pair of black bears and a margay, which is no longer seen in Texas. The zoo is also home to the very rare and endangered red wolf.

The zoo is shaded with pecan trees, and in the spring there is a wildflower exhibit that serves as a natural background to the native animals. Children will enjoy the "Zooboose," a railroad caboose that exhibits endangered animals. School districts and youth groups often visit the Texas Zoo, and the staff provides educational programs on a variety of topics.

Admission to this official "National Zoo of Texas" is free for children 12 and under and only $1 for those 13 and over. It is open daily, except for Thanksgiving, Christmas, and New Year's Day, from 10:00 A.M. to 5:00 P.M., and it stays open until 6:00 P.M. from May to August.

Westcave Preserve [HC]
45 minutes west of Austin
FM 3238
210-825-3442

This pristine preserve is an ecological system all its own, with 30 acres representing two ecosystems: grasslands, with ash and live oaks, and limestone formations, with cypress trees. Although it is virtually untouched by humans, it wasn't always that way. Back in the 1970s, the site was littered with trash. Today the policy is to tread lightly and take only pictures. Tours are available on Saturdays and Sundays at 10:00 A.M., noon, 2:00, and 4:00 P.M., year-round, weather permitting. Group tours of no more than 30 people are available during the week. There is no fee, but donations are accepted.

Chapter Seven

❧

Nature Study, Environmental Protection, & Volunteer Opportunities

S tudying, cleaning up, and volunteering may not sound like the types of activities kids relish, but don't let these terms turn them off from participating in these enjoyable and interesting opportunities. Learning and helping can really be a ton of fun, especially in an informal, outdoor setting. In addition, when children come away with new knowledge or the satisfaction of contributing to a good cause, the experience will be more meaningful and fulfilling. Some of the programs and facilities in this chapter are suited for individual children or families, while others work better for groups and schools, and most are appropriate for both families and groups.

Nature and Natural History Study

In addition to the programs and facilities listed in this chapter, many communities have small nature centers, museums, and botanical gardens that offer classes to local children during the school year and summer. Also look over chapter 2 and the overnight camps section in chapter 8 for more opportunities in nature and natural history study. The listings in this section are divided into programs and places.

Programs

Adopt-A-Wetland
Texas A&M University Corpus Christi
Center for Coastal Studies
Corpus Christi, TX 78418
512-980-3200

This program trains leaders and teachers on how their youth group or class can "adopt-a-wetland" in their community. Students learn to monitor a wetland area by studying it, testing waters, and observing plants and animals that live there. The program is free and can be integrated into curricula for grades K through 12.

Community Outreach Program
Darlene Lewis, Grant Director
Texas Parks & Wildlife Department
4200 Smith School Road
Austin, TX 78744

This innovative program began in 1996 as a means of enabling minority children and those in need or of nontraditional status to experience state parks and outdoor education and recreation. The program offers grants to cities and groups that are striving to expand wilderness adventure and exploration to the inner city. Call for application information.

Exploring Texas
Texas Parks & Wildlife
4200 Smith School Road

Austin, TX 78744
512-389-4362
http//www.tpwd.state.tx.us/expltx/intro/indexhtm

Looking for a class or group project that will challenge children to explore their local environment and sharpen technological skills as well? That is the idea behind this new program from Texas Parks & Wildlife. Exploring Texas is an opportunity to get children involved with their community by working on long-term projects investigating their local natural resources.

The ideas are student-generated but the project must fall into one of three categories: a descriptive project about the natural or cultural resources in their area; a project for which the class performs a service in the community dealing with natural resources; or an in-depth analysis of a current issue. Students may select the topic and form. For instance, the topic may be about a nature trail the class is building or a study of a local bat colony, and the project may include a timeline or oral history. In conjunction with the project, students design a web page using the information they have gathered. Web pages from across the state will eventually be connected, and students and adults will be able to take a closer look at different regions of the state through the children's eyes.

The Federal Junior Duck Stamp Conservation Program
Federal Duck Stamp Office
1849 C St., NW, Suite 2058
Washington, DC 20240
202-208-4354
Fax: 202-208-6296

This federal program was instituted to stop the destruction of wetlands that are breeding and nesting grounds for waterfowl. The Migratory Bird Hunting Stamp Act, passed in 1934, requires waterfowl hunters over 16 to purchase and carry a Federal Duck

Stamp. About 98 cents of every $1 of the stamp's price goes to purchasing wetlands for the National Wildlife Refuge System. Today collectors and conservationists are as apt as hunters to purchase the stamps, to help restore wetlands and because of the stamps' beauty and growth in value.

The Federal Junior Duck Stamp Conservation and Design Program began in 1989, and the Federal Junior Duck Stamp Conservation and Design Act was passed in 1994. The revenue from the sale of Junior Duck Stamps allows the U.S. Fish and Wildlife Service to promote conservation education by offering awards and scholarships to students, teachers, and schools that participate in the program. Students in kindergarten through high school can take part in this educational program in their schools, then they may enter the annual stamp art competition in Texas. The goal is to design a winning duck stamp. The Best of Show winning designer then competes at the national level in Washington, D.C. The national winner will see his or her design on the next year's Junior Duck Stamp.

Ocean in Motion—Texas State Aquarium's Traveling Exhibition
P.O. Box 331307
Corpus Christi, TX 78463-1307
1-800-477-GULF

Some children have never had the opportunity to visit the coast and take in the wonders of life on the beach and in the sea. Ocean in Motion is an award-winning exhibit aimed at introducing third and fourth graders across the state to sea life and marine wildlife conservation. This traveling 48-foot trailer visits schools, fairs, and special events and is a hit with all ages. Students circulate through the exhibit six at a time and learn about animals, pollution, marine-related industries, and artificial reefs from five modules. When the ship whistle blows, kids advance to a new area. The exhibit is popular because it houses live animals and loads of interactive bells-and-whistles displays.

Schools interested in Ocean in Motion must cover the cost of bringing it to their town or they can work with the Aquarium's grant writer, who will help them secure funds to pay for the exhibit. Call the Texas State Aquarium's Education Department at 512-881-1204 for scheduling and information.

Project WILD/Aquatic WILD
Texas Parks & Wildlife Department
4200 Smith School Road
Austin, TX 78744
512-389-4999

Through this nationally recognized program, teachers can learn how to teach environmental and wildlife studies and ecology in the classroom or with youth groups through six-hour training workshops. The activities they learn are hands-on and can be adapted for all levels and integrated into other curricula. The program is free and includes teacher-tested handbooks.

Texas State Aquarium's "Wonder Under the Sea"
P.O. Box 331307
Corpus Christi, TX 78463-1307
1-800-477-GULF

Teachers can enjoy television shows about marine life and the Gulf of Mexico environment filmed at the Texas State Aquarium and at other locations around the state. The programs are developed in cooperation with HEB food stores and are filmed by the local PBS affiliate, KEDT. PBS stations broadcast the show across the nation to thirty-nine other states. Teachers may also pick up the program via satellite directly into their classrooms.

The aquarium experts host the show with the help of local children. Experts from other institutions are often guests, and students may call a 1-800 line at the end of the program and talk to aquarium staff and ask questions. The shows airs once a month, and teachers may receive a curriculum packet with suggested activities that tie in with each show.

Texas Wildlife Association
1635 N.E. Loop 410, No. 108
San Antonio, TX 78209
210-826-2904

This association serves as an advocate of wildlife and the rights of wildlife managers, landowners, and hunters. They work to promote these interests through education, scientific study, and legislation. The association works with Texas Wildlife Forever, Inc., to integrate nature study involving wildlife into school curricula. Texas Wildlife Association sponsors youth participation in outdoor education, hunting, and fishing, and supports Project Wild among other programs.

Texas Wildlife Association offers special memberships to children. The Youth Level is for youngsters through 7th grade. They receive a special quarterly youth publications. The Student Level is for full-time students from 8th grade through college levels. These members may attend meetings but cannot vote.

Places

Aquarena Center [HC]
1 Aquarena Springs Drive
San Marcos, TX 78666
512-245-7534

Once called Aquarena Springs, this center dispensed with the lighter trappings when guardianship of the property transferred to Southwest Texas State University. The kids may miss the sky ride and swimming pig, but there is still plenty of wet fun and much to learn at the center. The center offers seven tours, all of which include a good dose of nature watching and study.

The Glass Bottom Boat Tour is likely to be a hit with kids. They can glide across the crystal-clear waters of 1,000 springs that form the headwaters of the San Marcos River. The lake is home to five endangered species, including the San Marcos dwarf salamander and the fountain darter. There is also a special boat tour that explores the endangered species in more depth. The Ecological Tour comes with a study guide and Aqua-Ranger Field Kit that includes water sampling tools, binoculars, a magnifying glass, maps, and activities.

The center is open year-round and children get a discounted rate. Tours for children run from $1 to $5.25 each. Group tours are available, along with banquet and meeting rooms.

Camp Sea World—Day Camp [HC]
Sea World of Texas
10500 Sea World Drive
San Antonio, TX 78521
210-523-3608   Fax: 210-523-3299
Director—Mary Alice Ramirez

What a great place to go to day camp. At Sea World Camp, kids ages 3 to 18 can enjoy the attractions of Sea World and learn about marine animals and the environment. Campers are divided into groups according to grade level and participate in activities geared for their age. Every group explores the animals in the park, learning about such topics as their habitats, environment, and adaptations, then visits the show featuring the particular animal it has studied. The camp offers fun activities as well, including crafts, games, songs, and cool dips in Shamu's Happy Harbor during hikes across the park. Friday night is leisure time. Students get to ride all the park's attractions, and younger kids camp out at the shark or penguin exhibits. Older students stay in dorms.

The camp can only take 150 children per session and it is very popular. Weekly sessions, Monday through Friday, start the first week of June and run through August. Call in early May to register for a specific week.

CCA/CPL Marine Development Center [GC]
4300 Waldron Rd.
Corpus Christi, TX 78418
512-939-7784

This development center is one of the largest marine hatcheries in the world. Since 1983, the center has managed to produce billions of redfish eggs and millions of trout eggs. Kids can see redfish and speckled trout in three-thousand-gallon saltwater spawning tanks where spawning is controlled by water temperature and lighting. They then follow the spawning process to the incubation room and rearing ponds. Tours are conducted at 1:00 P.M. and 3:00 P.M. on Tuesdays and Thursdays and at 10:00 A.M. and 2:00 P.M. on Saturdays. Interested school and youth groups can arrange special tours.

This center also sponsors an annual "Children's Fish-a-thon Event" which benefits the American Cancer Society. Children fish in privately stocked tanks for redfish and other species and take a tour of the facilities. There are prizes for both the best fundraisers and those who caught the biggest fish. The event typically takes place in April. Call for registration information.

Sea Center Texas [PL]
300 Medical Dr.
Lake Jackson, TX 77566
409-292-0100

This aquarium, marine development, and educational center is an effort by TPW, Dow North America, and the Coastal Conservation Association (CCA). The center is a hatchery capable of producing 20 million redfish and spotted seatrout fingerlings annually. It has 35 rearing ponds, a saltwater marsh demonstration project, and a hatchery building. Children will enjoy the "Touch Tank," where they can feel live crabs, sea urchins, and sea anemones.

The center's aquariums are a popular draw as well. Each represents a different level of life in the Gulf, starting with the Salt Marsh Aquarium featuring bait fish, killifish, and fiddler crabs. Next is the Coastal Bay exhibit, which replicates life around and under a pier. The Jetties display features granite rocks jutting out into the water, and the Artificial Reef and Gulf exhibits show marine life in the open waters, with tropical fish, grouper, snapper red drum, and sharks. Individuals can tour without reservations. Groups should call ahead for the Hatchery Tour. The center's hours are Tuesday through Friday, 9:00 A.M.–4:00 P.M., Saturday, 10:00 A.M.–5:00 P.M., and Sunday, 1:00–4:00 P.M. Admission is free.

Vanishing Texas River Cruise [HC]
P.O. Box 901
Burnet, TX 78611
512-756-6986
1-800-728-8735

During the winter, the Vanishing Texas River Cruise gives people the opportunity to view the eagles that make their home at Lake Buchanan. Children can expect to see eagles during November through mid-March and many other types of birds and wildlife as well all year round. Ospreys, red-tailed hawks, pelicans, deer, and turkey are common sights on this tour. Guides narrate the trip, relating information about eagle habitats, local ecology, and conservation. Admission is $15 for adults, $13 for seniors and kids 13 through college, $10 for kids age 6–12, and free for children 5 and under.

School and youth groups can take a special tour at discounted prices. The students receive a questionnaire workbook and must listen closely to the narration to get the answers. The tour guide gives the teacher or leader a book with the answers. The boat can hold up to 200 people and has two upper observation decks. The bottom deck is enclosed, with heating and air conditioning. The tour offers complimentary water, tea, and coffee. All tours last 2 ½ hours from 11:00 A.M.–1:30 P.M. Don't forget binoculars and cameras, and dress in layers during the fall and winter. Call for reservations.

Welder Wildlife Foundation [GC]
P.O. Box 1400
Sinton, TX 78387
512-364-2643
Fax: 512-364-2650

Located north of Sinton on US 77, the Welder Wildlife Refuge is the largest privately endowed wildlife refuge in the world. Provisions for the refuge are provided by the estate of late rancher Rob Welder. Families may take a tour of the refuge from 3:00 to 5:00 P.M. on Thursdays for free, and special workshops are scheduled throughout the year on specific topics.

The backbone of the refuge is research and education, and the staff works with school classes, Scouts, 4-H, and nature conservancy groups to meet their individual needs. If a biology class is studying insects, for instance, the class would use the refuge as a research area, collecting species, identifying them, and examining their relationship with plants and other animals. The refuge will also provide a more general experience for a group with a tour on wetland ecology or wildlife management.

The group tours and study are free unless students stay overnight, when there is a $3 per student fee. The Welder Foundation has a dormitory that sleeps up to 36 students and includes kitchen facilities. Groups must provide and cook their own meals.

Wild Basin Wilderness Preserve [HC]
805 Capital of Texas Highway
Austin, TX 78746
512-327-7622

Good things are close to home—like this 227-acre preserve in Austin. Not only can kids hike the trails and woods, they can also study plants and animals with experts in botany, geology, birding, tracking, flint knapping, and entomology. During the school year, students arrive by the busload. The preserve is ready for them with programs geared for kindergarten-age kids through upper elementary-age students. The preserve is home to two endangered birds—the golden-cheeked warbler and the black-capped vireo. There are four miles of hiking trails and one has wheelchair access.

The preserve is on Loop 360, 1¼ miles north of Bee Cave Rd. Tours are open to the public, and members receive a discount on admission. Students who join the preserve for $15 will receive a newsletter. Call or write for a current calendar.

State and National Parks Nature Programs

State and national parks offer a wide variety of programs and classes for children. Before visiting one, call and ask if they have special days or programs for kids. The parks listed here have conducted children's day camps or classes in the past. These are subject to change and additional programs may be instituted at other parks as well. Check with the individual park before making plans.

George Observatory—Brazos Bend State Park [GC]
U.S. Hwy. 59
Rt. 1, Box 840
Neddville, TX 77461
409-553-5101

On Saturdays, future astronomers and their families can visit this working observatory and Challenger Learning Center dedicated to the memory of the seven Challenger astronauts. Students work together to solve problems and complete a shuttle mission. Kids can use telescopes and visit the exhibits. At 5:00 P.M., everyone gets a free pass to the main dome, where the 36-inch telescope is located. The observatory is open from 3:00 to 10:00 P.M.

Eisenhower State Park [PL]
Rt. 2, Box 50K

Denison, TX 75020
Contact: Chris True, 903-465-1956 or 903-463-4790

School and youth groups can work with this park and custom
design a program around a topic they are studying. Popular ones
in the past include wildlife, fossils, and bats, but rangers will work
to integrate others as well. The park features an amphitheater set
in the woods that holds 150 kids. After the program, groups can
hike through six miles of trails, including a self-guided nature
trail. Printed guides are available in the office with information
on local flora and fauna. Guided tours are sometimes given as
well. Spring is the most popular time of year, so call in advance to
book a program.

Junior Ranger Program [PL]
Washington-On-The-Brazos State Historical Park
Superintendent
P.O. Box 305
Washington, TX 77880
409-878-2214

This park has a well-established Junior Ranger Program that is
in place each summer, usually running one month. Kids ages 6–12
attend Wednesday, Thursday, and Friday each week and study a
different subject each day, in the areas of natural history, inde-
pendence, and the environment. Participants might find themselves cooking in an 1850s kitchen with artifacts from that period one day and then heading out to the beaver pond to collect
insects or study birds the next. Children do not have to attend all
days or weeks, but those who do receive a Junior Ranger button
and other recognition. The fee is $3 per child per day.

The park also gives guided 30-minute tours to school groups
and offers a variety of expanded programs around various historical and natural themes. Call for a detailed listing of expanded
programs or to reserve a tour.

Wildlife Track Identification for Kids [SP]
Calliham Unit, Choke Canyon State Park
Park Superintendent
P.O. Box 2, Calliham, TX 78007
512-786-3868

Kids ages 6 to 12 can take this morning class at various times of the year. A conservation specialist guides the children in a walk on the shore of Choke Canyon Lake looking for and identifying animal tracks. Later, students learn how to make plaster of paris prints to save their tracks. The class runs from 9:00 A.M. to noon, and reservations are required.

National Parks

Padre Island National Seashore [GC]
Junior Seashore Ranger Program and the
    Sea Star Discovery Program
9405 South Padre Island Dr.
Corpus Christi, TX 78418-5597
512-949-8068
25 miles south of the JFK Causeway on Park Rd. 22, outside Corpus Christi

The National Seashore stretches over eighty miles on the north end of Padre Island. At the entrance is Malaquite Beach, the only developed area in the park, where the park rangers conduct classes for the Junior Seashore Ranger Program. Classes take place each Saturday throughout the year, with additional days in the summer. Children may attend one or two classes or complete a series of classes to earn a ranger patch and badge. Summer visitors can complete the series over a long weekend or through a week, and the program works well for clubs and youth groups, too.

Classes are for children ages 5 through 13, and topics vary, but are tied to exploring, studying, and protecting the beach, dunes, water, and indigenous plants and animals. A sample of programs includes an introduction to island bird watching, hands-on workshops using scientific tools to measure water salinity and wind direction and speed, and nature walks on the beach and the edge of the dunes to identify wild animals from their tracks.

The Sea Star Discovery Program is for anyone, children through adults, and again is recommended for both individuals and groups. This self-guided adventure starts with picking up a package of material about a particular wildlife subject such as insects, tracking, birds, or plants. Participants use the park and a questionnaire to explore the subject and when the packet is complete, turn it in for bonus points. Bonus points add up to exciting fun and prizes. Kids or groups can earn field guides, posters, and even a boat trip out into the Laguna Madre.

In addition to these classes and programs, Malaquite Beach offers nature trails, a boardwalk, a covered pavilion, a snack bar, a self-guided indoor educational area, book and gift stores, and an auditorium which is often used for puppet shows. Both programs are free, but visitors must pay a $10 per vehicle entry fee into the park good for seven days, or $20 for an annual pass.

Big Thicket National Preserve [PW]
P.O. Box 7408
Beaumont, TX 77706
409-839-2689

This 86,000-acre preserve is known as "the biological crossroads of North America" because of the broad range of flora and fauna native to the area. Children will enjoy hiking, canoeing, and watching the abundance of wildlife. Unfortunately, this abundance includes mosquitoes, so remember to bring insect repellent.

Ask for the Junior Ranger Activity packet at the park's head-quarters. It comes with magnifiers, compass activity book, and collection jars. New to Big Thicket is its activity book, *Big Fun in the Big Thicket,* with several hours of fun and informative activities about the preserve, including puzzles and games for learning about plant and animal identification and local geography.

The heart of the children's educational program at the Big Thicket Preserve is the planned school and youth group visits. Although open to any group across the state, the preserve sees many groups from its immediate geographical area. The rangers will work with the teachers or leaders to determine the group's needs and objectives and then design a tour and program tailored to fit the school's objectives. The rangers are prepared to deal with children in grades pre-K through college, although their focus is on the intermediate grades.

There is no fee for this program, and they will take a maximum of 110 youngsters at a time. Rangers stress that they *require* a ratio of one adult for every ten children so they may run a controlled lesson. Rangers also recommend that teachers borrow their intro-duction videotape that lays out the preserve's objectives and methods of operation so they will be prepared for their visit. A school representative should call 409-246-2377 at least two weeks before the planned outing to discuss the type of program they want.

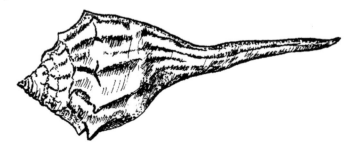

Volunteer Work and Environmental Clean-up and Protection Efforts

Nothing instills appreciation of the natural world like getting your hands dirty while maintaining and preserving it. Many organizations that work to preserve, maintain, and repair wildlife areas are nonprofit and rely heavily on volunteers of all ages. By volunteering, children learn what an enormous task it is to balance human life and wildlife. Kids will feel a sense of satisfaction with a job well done and gain valuable training for the future.

In addition to these listings, children can volunteer for city and school programs or at local nature centers and arboretums. Also contact the centers and museums listed in chapter 2. These types of institutions are generally nonprofit and rely heavily on volunteers. Many, like the Texas State Aquarium and the Dallas Museum of Natural Science, offer specific training programs and jobs for kids and teens.

Adopt-A-Beach
Texas General Land Office
4204 Woodcock Drive, Ste. 240
San Antonio, TX 78228-1324
1-800-85-BEACH

The purpose of this program is to clean Texas beaches and educate people on how they can prevent polluting them in the first place. Twice a year, in October and April, volunteers from across the state emerge on the Gulf shores to pick up and record debris. Since 1986, more than 180,000 volunteers collected more than 3,640 tons of trash. Thousands of kids participate annually, and the program is open to school classes, youth groups, families, and individuals.

A second part of this program involves a statewide children's art contest created so children can express their love of and involvement with beaches. Each November, the commission sends out invitations for entries to all Texas public schools with grades K through 6. The kids are asked to show through their art what the treasures of the coast mean to them. Individuals and students in home schooling or private schools may also enter. From the thousands of entries, a panel picks 48 winners, two from each council of government across the state. The panel then visits the schools and recognizes the winners. The grand prize winner receives an expenses-paid trip to the beach for his or her class. The classroom teacher gets to go with the class and receives a separate trip as well. Corporate sponsors are always needed to help fund this program.

Clean Texas 2000 Partnership Section
Texas Natural Resource Conservation Commission
P.O. Box 13087
Austin, TX 78711-3087
512-239-3150

Clean Texas 2000 is for individuals, groups, businesses, local governments, and schools that are interested in reducing waste and preventing pollution in the state. To become a member, the child, class, school, or group must submit one or more environmental projects to Clean Texas 2000. They will then become a Partner and receive a certificate signed by the governor and the chairman of the TNRCC.

The governor recognizes the most outstanding partnership projects annually. There are special award categories for "Education" and "Youth." The winners are honored at a banquet in Austin.

Environmental Challenge
Texas General Land Office
4204 Woodcock Drive, Ste. 240
San Antonio, TX 78228-1324
1-800-832-8224 or
512-463-5339

The HEB grocery company sponsors this environmental program, and the Texas General Land Office administers it. The program started in 1989 as a contest with nine awards, but developed
into a successful grant program. The office now grants a total of
$25,000 to schools across the state in increments that range from
$100 to $750. They generally receive close to 500 applications
and select just under 40 recipients.

The purpose of the program is to recognize classes that develop hands-on community-linked environmental projects. Past
winners have included a park clean-up program that was adopted
by the local city council, and a science class that traveled to Big
Bend to study the causes and effects of air pollution in that area.

Interested teachers must complete a short application in
October and grants are announced in December. Judges look for
projects that go beyond the mundane and that have community
significance or tackle a major environmental issue.

The Nature Conservancy of Texas
P.O. Box 1440
San Antonio, TX 78295-1440
210-224-8774
http://www.tnc.org/texas

The Nature Conservancy of Texas is dedicated to protecting
wildlife and acquiring land to set up preserves. There are volun-

teer opportunities for youth and school groups in six regions throughout the state. Primarily these opportunities involve maintenance work on one of over thirty preserves. The best way to find opportunities in a particular area is to call for a map and list of upcoming volunteer jobs.

> Student Conservation Association (SCA) High School
>   Conservation Work Crew Program
> SCA Recruiting Department
> P.O. Box 550
> Charlestown, NH 03603-0550
> 603-543-1700
> e-mail: internships@sca~inc.org

SCA volunteer opportunities are for older students who are serious about working in and learning about the environment and natural wilderness. They should expect to put in *hard physical work* performing tasks such as reconstructing or clearing trails and revegetating wilderness areas. Teens will camp and live with a small group and crew leaders.

This program requires students to complete an application and have a teacher, administrator, or coach complete one as well. Physically able students age 16 through graduating senior status may apply. Texas is in region 8. Call or write for an application and more information.

State Park Volunteers

For a listing of state parks, contact TPW at 1-800-792-1112.

Youth groups such as the Boy Scouts of America, 4-H Clubs, and school classes make a significant contribution to state park research and study each year. Jobs are as varied as collecting data, sketching, taking photos, and cataloging. Contact the state park you are interested in helping.

Texas Hummerbird Round-Up
Texas Parks and Wildlife Department
4200 Smith School Road
Austin, TX 78744
1-800-792-1112

Help a child take part in this volunteer survey in your own backyard. Volunteers receive a package that includes a survey form, educational tools, and flower seeds to produce plants that will attract hummingbirds in the spring. Also included are tips for attracting the birds, information, and a map of the "Texas Ten" showing where the rare and unusual species have been sighted.

To sign up, send a legal-sized self-addressed stamped envelope that includes your county name and a $5 donation payable to TPWD Nongame Fund to the above address.

The Texas Monarch Watch
Texas Parks & Wildlife Department
c/o Nongame & Urban Wildlife Program
4200 Smith School Road
Austin, TX 78744
Call: The Monarch Hotline at 1-800-468-9719 or
512-326-2231.

The Texas Monarch Watch is a volunteer program designed to track and count monarch butterflies two times a year: as they migrate from Canada through Texas for the winter, and when they return from Mexican wintering grounds in the spring. The Monarch Watch strives to promote science education, particularly in elementary and secondary schools, to promote conservation of the butterflies, and to involve people in cooperative research. Individuals, families, and school classes can join the watch for $10.

Volunteers keep a daily calendar of how many monarchs are in their area. Other activities include raising or capturing and tagging butterflies to track them. Observation is usually over a specific two-day period.

Texas Watch
Texas Natural Resource Conservation Commission
P.O. Box 13087
Austin, TX 78711-3087
512-239-4741
or
Texas Parks & Wildlife Department
4200 Smith School Road
Austin, TX 78744
1-800-792-1112

Texas Watch is a volunteer monitoring program that encourages people to keep track of water quality. The program is a team effort between TPW and the Texas Natural Resource Conservation Commission. Students make up 40% of this program's 5,000 volunteers. The purpose in involving students is to gather important data and, at the same time, introduce students to water-quality concepts and how various factors influence the quality of Texas waters. Schools and interested groups can receive training to help develop a monitoring program.

U.S. Fish & Wildlife Service
Region 2
Volunteer Coordinator
P.O. Box 1306

Gold Avenue, SW Room 1306
Albuquerque, NM 87103

The U.S. Fish and Wildlife Service uses volunteers in its wildlife refuges and fisheries across the nation, including in Texas. Volunteers might do such varied work as conducting fish population surveys, leading tours, photographing natural resources, performing clerical duties, and banding birds. Anyone can volunteer, but those under the age of 18 must have written parental approval. The service encourages youngsters under 16 years old to volunteer in adult-led groups like school clubs, 4-H, or Scouts. Write or call for specific information and addresses of refuges and fisheries.

United States Youth Conservation Corps
U.S. Department of Agriculture
Forest Service
Washington,DC 20090-6090
or
U.S. Department of the Interior
Fish and Wildlife Service
Washington, DC 20240

This program is an opportunity for young people ages 15 through 18 to work and earn money on projects that help develop and maintain our natural resources. There are two programs: residential and nonresidential. Students interested in nonresidential programs will work in areas within a short commute of their homes. Residential volunteers will live in a camp for 5–7 days a week for the entire summer program. A minimal charge for room and board will be deducted from students' pay. Kids can expect to participate in such projects as constructing trails, building camping facilities, planting trees, and clearing areas. Ask for an application from the above addresses or through regional Fish and Wildlife Services, Park Services, or school counselors.

VIPs—Volunteers in National Parks

Contact the VIP coordinator from the national park in which you want to volunteer. Generally, volunteer work in national parks is done by adults, but minors (under age 18) may volunteer in parks in their community if they get the official permission of their parents. To volunteer outside the community, kids will need to be with their family or in a supervised group.

Chapter Eight

Overnight Camps & Trips

O vernight camps and trips give children the opportunity to immerse themselves in outdoor activities. Although many traditional camps offer some type of nature study and outdoor exploration, the following camps and trips make it their primary focus.

The trips and excursions listed are for kids who live in Texas who want to see the outside world in other parts of Texas or the United States. Several of the overnight camps also offer trips and some will specially design trips for a specific youth group. Other good sources for overnight nature travel include church groups, school clubs, youth organizations, and sports clubs. The ones listed here are for older children and teens and center around travel to state and national parks or other natural areas.

Before sending a child to any camp or on any trip, it pays to check out the program thoroughly first. Get references from friends or prior campers and visit the facilities if possible. Even if you select an excellent camp or trip, make sure it is suitable for your child. Age appropriateness and camp descriptions are given to help you select one right for your child.

American Camping Association

The ACA is a national organization that includes about one third of all camps in the United States. The association accredits and inspects member camps at least once every three years to ensure they are high-quality programs. In addition, they certify camp directors. Camps with the ACA certification are not guaranteed to be perfect camps, but the certification is one assurance that they have been evaluated by an outside organization using national standards.

C.A.M.P.

C.A.M.P. stands for Camping Association for Mutual Progress and is an organization of camps primarily in Texas that work with state government to set laws associated with camps. One effort attributed to this group, together with the Boy Scouts of America, was the push to establish the high standards used by the Texas Health Department when inspecting camps,

Backpacking Camp—Austin Nature Center [HC]
301 Nature Center Dr.
Austin, TX 78746
512-327-8181
Contact: Rachel Moyer

This backpacking camp takes kids ages 11 through 13 to hike and camp across trails at various locations. Past trips included backpacking in Bastrop State Park and Lost Maples State Park. Campers learn how to pack for a backpacking trip, how to set up camp, and how to cook outdoors, as well as survival skills and first aid. The center provides gear, transportation, and food. The camp includes two overnight camp-outs and runs $150–$175 per camper. This nature center offers a wide variety of outdoor experiences for children. For further information on its programs, see chapter 2, page 14.

Bobwhite Brigade [PP]
Texas Agricultural Extension Service
7887 N. Hwy. 87
San Angelo, TX 76901
Director—Dr. Dale Rollins

This education-intensive four-day camp is for 28 boys and girls ages 15-17 who have at least a 3.0 grade point average. In a secluded ranch in Haskell County, wildlife professionals work with teens each summer, teaching them ecology and natural resource management. The camp hopes to inspire young leaders and, particularly, to teach quail conservation.

Bobwhite Brigade is the effort of many agencies and businesses, including the Texas Agricultural Extension Service, Quail Unlimited, Texas Parks & Wildlife, the Soil Conservation Service, Krooked River Outfitters, and local conservation districts.

Kids begin the camping session by taking a pre-test and then start hands-on study. Campers are divided into small groups called "coveys" that work together with a biologist to learn quail habitats and management. Evenings are spent shooting clay targets and shotgunning. Each "covey" makes oral presentations and is awarded points for the best management plans. There is a Top Covey Award for the most points earned. After camp is over,

teens continue their study through the next year and the one that has the most distinguished record of activity pertaining to the camp is awarded a $500 scholarship.

Camp Lone Star [PL]
2016 Camp Lone Star Road
La Grange, TX 78945
409-247-4128 or 800-362-2078
lonestar@cvtv.net
Director—Garland Midgett

This summer camp is owned by the Lutheran Outdoors Ministry of Texas but is open to everyone. Although it is a religious camp, the camp's director says that they use their natural environment instead of the pulpit to pass on their message. The camp offers a wide variety of outdoor activities, including archery, camp fires, fishing, hiking, trap range, and swimming. In addition, campers may get a chance to canoe down the Colorado, San Marcos, or Guadalupe Rivers or take offshore fishing excursions and special backpacking trips.

The Children's Camp runs from the first of June through early August in five- and two-day sessions. Campers may combine one or more sessions as well. The summer camp is open to kids ages 5 to 18; the kids are divided by age and experience age-appropriate activities. Five-day sessions run $259 and two-day camps cost $99. Discounts are available for groups, those combining two or more camps, or families sending more than one person.

Camp Lone Star will also rent out its facilities to all types of groups and can provide staff to teach outdoor activities. They have an extensive challenge course and ropes course for summer camp or for groups and can also arrange guided trips.

Each year, the Lutheran Outdoors Ministry offers eco-travel trips to various areas in Texas through both Camp Lone Star and the Texoma Lutheran Camp. Trips may vary, but Lone Star hosts a Family Fishing trip to the Gulf of Mexico, for instance. They make arrangements with a motel on the coast and charter boats, and interested families register and meet for a fishing trip in the Gulf, bay fishing, and shrimp and crab boils.

Camp Sea World—Careers Program [HC]
Sea World of Texas
10500 Sea World Drive
San Antonio, TX 78521
210-523-3608
Fax: 210-523-3299
Director—Mary Alice Ramirez ACA

Sea World park is the exciting location for Sea World Camp. This environmental education program is for teens in grades 9 though 12 who want to explore marine-related careers. Teens work with all the animals, including dolphins, sea lions, killer whales, and sharks, for a week. Along with marine center activities, counselors teach leadership training and academic and environmental education. Of course, there's a lot of swimming and water fun throughout the park, too.

Camp sessions are held during spring break, the summer, and fall. Each session can hold 20 to 40 children, but campers are advised to register and fill out their applications early. For summer camp, students should start applying in early April since many sessions may be closed by May. Entrance is based on the students' written essays explaining their interest in marine biology and why they should be accepted. In addition, the students must send two letters of recommendation from teachers or counselors which confirm their sincere interest in marine biological sciences.

The camp is coed, and students stay in on-site dormitories. Cost is $500 to $700 for an eight-day session (Saturday to Saturday). Tuition covers all meals and student supplies. The camp picks up the campers from the airport and delivers them to it.

Caney Creek Fishing Camp [GC]
2603 Augusta Dr.
Houston, TX 77057
713-780-1471
Owner—Chuck Duff

Go fish! This special summer camp is for boys ages 8 to 18 who want to fish the summer days away. Caney Creek, located on the east end of east Matagorda Bay, hires a college student each year whom they train to become a boat captain. The licensed boat captain then takes kids fishing in the bays for trout, redfish, and flounder on a 22-foot boat. Kids stay in the marina apartment which serves as a dorm with bunk beds, but spend most of their time on the water. They are up at 6:00 A.M., in the boat by 7:00, and fish until noon. The boat brings them back for lunch and rest and napping until 4:00 P.M., when they get up and hit the water again until dark.

Boys can sign up for two days to a week, and the cost per day is $125. The camp provides a boat and captain, lodging, meals, and equipment. Boys younger than 8 may attend either a father-son camp or a family camp. Caney Creek has taken girls on a family or mother-daughter basis in the past and hopes to expand a program to girls in the future.

Conservation Camp [HC]
Fossil Rim State Park
PO Box 2189
Glenrose, TX 76043
254-897-2960

This taste of Africa in the Texas Hill country is located on over 2,700 acres and features dozens of exotic and endangered animals to view. The ranch participates in the Species Survival Plan, which is a worldwide managed-conservation program that serves as a breeding ground for endangered species. These include two kinds of rhinoceros, Grevy's zebra, cheetah, oryx, addax antelope, and three types of wolves.

Take your family, youth group, or science club on a special day and overnight Conservation Camp at Fossil Rim. The overnight is becoming popular for family reunions as well. A nature guide will take you in a Land Rover to see areas that drive-through tourists don't get to see. You'll take nature hikes and get a closer look at the animals. Both camps also feature safari tours, small animal presentations, and fossil hunts. Overnight campers take night hikes and enjoy a camp fire, then spend the night in a screened bunkhouse. Day camp runs from 9:00 A.M. until 4:00 P.M., and overnight camp starts at 1:00 P.M. one day and ends at 11:00 A.M. the next day. Fossil Rim can handle all size groups, but call as early as possible to make reservations—at least 3 to 4 weeks ahead of time.

The overnight camp costs $58 per person for groups of 10–23, and $52 per person for groups of 24 or more. The fee includes dinner and breakfast. Bring a sleeping bag. For more adventurous camping you can bring your own tent and receive a discount of $10.

A Wilderness Camp is in the planning. This camp will include a five-mile guided hike to a remote campsite. Tents are provided, but you need to bring sleeping bags and backpacks. Call for prices and availability. Camps are open year-round.

Hamman Ranch YMCA [HC]
Mike Dawson
HC 01 Box 710
Bandera, TX 78003
800-531-5694
830-796-7449

This coed camp is open to preteens and teens ages 11–16. Because they limit the age, the camp is smaller, taking about 65 to 70 campers in one- and two-week sessions. Campers attending the regular camp session can expect to ride horseback, rock climb, rappel, and canoe in the Medina River. The camp also offers a high ropes challenge course, cave exploration, swimming, and night gazing through telescopes at stars, planets, and the moon. Kids who opt for the second week spend it taking in-depth day trips canoeing or rock climbing. A unique feature of this camp is that campers stay in Native American-inspired teepees built on platforms. Tuition for one week runs $315 and for two weeks, $475.

Hamman Ranch also holds specialty camps in the summer in which campers choose one interest to explore. Campers who choose Horsemanship Camp are assigned a horse to feed, saddle, groom, and ride at least three hours a day. Young shooters may earn their Texas Hunter's Certification at Marksmanship Camp, where they practice with 22's, deer rifles, skeet, blackpowder muzzle loaders, and archery. A popular camp is Hill Country Adventure Camp, which takes kids on a 3-day rock and rappelling trip to Enchanted Rock and a 2-day canoeing trip on the Guadalupe River.

For long-distance travel, teens can opt for one of the trip camps. One trip explores North Arkansas, with canoeing on the Buffalo National River and spelunking in five caves at Devil's Den State Park. The other adventure takes campers to Taylor Park in Colorado, for ten days of rafting and rock climbing along with a three-day backpacking trip. Inquire about new trips each year.

Hamman Ranch sponsors a special family camp for three days in two sessions during the 4th of July weekend. During the school year school groups may book the camp for outdoor education. Currently the curriculum is geared for 5th and 6th grade and studies include astronomy, biology, cave study, and advanced camping skills.

John Knox Ranch [HC]
Star Route 1, Box 12
Fischer, TX 78623
830-935-4568
Directors—Heidi and Mike McFalls

This camp, owned by Mission Presbytery, is located on the Blanco River west of Canyon Lake. Although it is a religious camp, there are no requirements in order to attend, and the staff welcomes all children in grades rising to third through tenth. The camp emphasizes community, working, living, and playing together, and strives to make each camper feel part of a group.

Many of the activities at the camp are centered around the 300 acres of hill country wilderness which includes the river and a spring-fed creek with a blue swimming hole. Campers can rock climb, rappel, canoe, swim, practice archery, hike, and participate in wilderness study. Each session includes an overnight camp-out under the stars where kids can really get the feel of living in the wild and cooking over a fire. Facilities at the camp are rustic, with cabins and an outdoor, covered pavilion for meals. Campers should bring sleeping bags. Sessions run one week, ten days, or two weeks and cost $250 for one week, $300 for ten days, and $390 for two weeks.

John Knox offers special travel and adventure camps as well. In the past, it has taken high school seniors water skiing on Canyon Lake and sailing in Rockport. Annually, it features four beach trips to the coast staying in Corpus Christi and a backpacking trip to Colorado. Another favorite is a ten-day trip to Big Bend to rock climb, rappel, and white-water raft. Call for more information.

Living Jungle Science Program Trips
3130 Waurika
San Antonio, TX 78223
210-337-3743
Fax: 1-210-337-5191

Living Jungle, with twenty-three years of experience, was one of the pioneers in planning and leading eco-tours in Texas. It emphasizes that this experience gives its programs quality and depth. Living Jungle offers ecological science trips to school districts during the summer and also assists science teachers in setting up ecological and science day camps and classes on their campus.

Although they can custom-design programs to suit a school's needs, two trips in Texas are scheduled each year. Living Jungle takes kids to Big Bend and the Guadalupe and Davis Mountains for an ecology field trip where they camp, visit the McDonald Observatory, and attend the evening bat flight program. The other annual trip is to the coast to study Gulf of Mexico marine biology. Campers will visit the Texas State Aquarium, the Aransas Wildlife Refuge, Galveston Island, and the National Marine Fisheries Center. Kids will fish during the day and observe wildlife at night. Every two to three years, Living Jungle also schedules a trip to Yosemite, Yellowstone, and the Grand Canyon that usually lasts about six days. Call for information, current schedule, and prices.

Outpost Wilderness Adventure [HC]
P.O. Box 511
Hunt, TX 78024
830-238-4383 or 830-238-4650
e-mail: hoh@owa.com
Contact: David Appleton

From September through May, the Heart O' The Hills camp facility in Hunt is available for school, youth, and church groups or families and includes the option of guided wilderness adventure activities. The experienced staff can outfit and lead youth groups in rock climbing, mountain biking, fly fishing, team building, alpine climbing, and back-country travel.

The camp sits on 150 acres, with the lodge perched on Pawnee Hill overlooking the Guadalupe River. The lodge features sixteen private rooms with baths, two suites, and a separate dorm building that sleeps 32 people. The facilities also include a lobby with a fireplace, meeting rooms, an outdoor amphitheater, two lighted tennis courts, and a dining room that seats 175. Meals are provided, but a group can choose to bring and cook their own as well. Pricing ranges from $20 to $60 per person, per day.

For adventure outside of Texas, ask about the Outpost travel program. Many kids from Texas travel to their base camp at the Tarryall Mountains in Colorado each summer to experience in-depth activities such as backpacking, mountain biking, rafting, rock climbing, and fly fishing. Outpost also arranges adventure travel for groups to more exotic locales like Ecuador, Alaska, the Alps, and Costa Rica. Call or write for available trips and pricing.

Parrie Haynes Ranch [HC]
Texas Parks & Wildlife Department
4200 Smith School Road
Austin, TX 78744
1-800-792-1112 or 817-554-4052

This special camp was conceived as a way to introduce outdoor activities to youths who wouldn't normally get the chance. Originally the land was willed to the orphans of Texas by Mrs. Parrie Haynes, and the Texas Youth Commission used it as a reha-bilitation facility for juvenile offenders. It didn't prove practical and eventually the Game Warden Association linked up with Texas Parks & Wildlife Foundation to establish an outdoor edu-cational center instead.

Campers get the highest quality instruction in shooting, archery, plant and animal study, canoeing, and water safety on a beautiful 4,400-acre ranch bordering the Lampasas River. Campers are selected through referrals from counselors, churches, and social workers. Consideration is given to low-income families and single-parent households. The camp is free.

Sea Camp [GC]
Texas A&M University at Galveston
Sea Camp Director
P.O. Box 1675
Galveston, TX 77553-1675
409-740-4525
e-mail: turrubia@tamug.tamu.edu
Director—Judy Wern

This popular camp is for children 10 to 17 years old who like the water and have an interest in marine science. Sponsored by Texas A&M University at Galveston, this week-long camp gives kids a chance to study marine life and the coastal environment hands-on.

Sea Camp I, the premier program, takes 10- to 12-year-olds and 13- and 14-year-olds to the salt marsh off West Galveston Bay and the Gulf beach front. Here they learn about the food chain, bird watch, collect oysters with a biologist, and trawl for shrimp, fish, and crabs from a research vessel.

Kids age 13 through 16 who have attended Sea Camp in the past and new campers age 14 to 16 enroll in Sea Camp II. They study the beach, marsh, mudflats, jetties, and the bay by beachcombing and bird and dolphin watching.

Sea Camp III is for teens age 14 to 16 who are interested in fishing and learning about fish. Kids learn to tie knots, cast better, try out lures, and seine for bait. They also visit a fish hatchery and a wholesale fish market.

Marine mammals take center stage at Sea Camp IV, for kids

age 15 to 17. Campers work with the Marine Mammal Stranding Network and the university to study a wide range of topics relating to marine mammals, from conservation to physiology.

Sea Camp V is a travel camp that takes teens from Sabine Pass down to the Padre Island National Seashore. Kids camp out on the beaches, canoe, trawl Aransas Bay, visit the Texas State Aquarium, and explore the Laguna Madre.

Finally, for those with a thirst for a foreign adventure, Sea Camp VI will take kids 16 and 17 to study ecology in Belize. Campers must have attended previous camps or have a teacher recommendation and undergo a telephone interview.

Sea Camp instructors are faculty members from the Department of Marine Biology at TAMUG and graduate students. Spaces are limited and fill up fast. Call or write for an application. Tuition for Sea Camp is: Camp I—$625; Camps II, III, IV, and V—$675; and Camp VI to Belize—$1,650.

Southwest Texas State University Aquatic Studies Camp [HC]
Edward's Research and Data Center
Southwest Texas State University
San Marcos, TX 78666
512-245-2329

Water lovers will dive in head first for this camp. It's for both boys and girls age 9–15. Youngsters are grouped according to age, with sessions for 9- to 11-year-olds, 11- to 13-year-olds, and 13- to 15-year-olds. Enrollment is limited to 26 people on a first-come-first-served basis for each of the nine sessions that run during the summer. Children study aquatic biology and water conservation using the natural resources of the San Marcos River and Edwards Aquifer. Half of the day is spent enjoying eco-sports and water activities like rafting, tubing, scuba diving, snorkeling, and swimming. Side trips include jaunts to Sea World and Natural Bridge Caverns. Tuition is $450, which includes six days of camp, room board, instruction, and activities.

Texoma Lutheran Camp [PL]
Route 1, Box 116-P
Potsboro, TX 75076
903-786-3121
888-886-6198
e-mail: lomtexoma@texoma.net
Director—Keith Lund

Texoma Lutheran Camp holds summer camp through June and July, and although the camp incorporates religious study, there is also a strong emphasis on nature. There's plenty of water and wilderness to explore on the 590-acre spread on Lake Texoma. Activities include fishing, hiking, outdoor living skills, challenge course, water skiing, ropes course, sailing, rappelling, and camp fires. Kids stay in cabins and camp out one night each session. Older kids paddle out to sandy islands in the lake and camp out.

In addition to eco-sports, the camp strives to teach children about the outdoors and nature by integrating Project Wild activities into the curriculum. These activities, such as "Predator and Prey" and "Frozen Critters," are active games and popular with the campers, who may not even realize that they are learning. Texoma Lutheran Camp takes 80 campers ages 5 through high school per session. Each session costs $259.

In addition to the regular summer camp, Texoma Lutheran simultaneously runs Specialty Camps, including West Way, centered around horseback riding, and Water Way, which emphasizes water skiing. Two other specialty camps take kids of various ages into the wild for a week. Campers who sign up for Operation Outpost hike through the woods and then build their own shelters and live in the wild for a week. The Trek camp takes kids canoeing starting from camp on the lake and then down the river. Along the way, they sleep, cook, and eat outdoors. Specialty camp fees run slightly higher than regular camp fees and vary in price, so call for current information.

During the school year, the camp offers Outdoors Education in one- to five-day camps for school groups. Many Lutheran schools and public schools from the Dallas and Houston areas already participate, but the camps are open to any school in Texas. Camps are designed in cooperation with the school, and teachers may choose from a list of activities.

YMCA Camp Flaming Arrow [HC]
Hunt, Texas 78024
830-238-4631
Director—Steven King ACA

In the pretty Hill Country 16 miles west of Kerrville, campers stay on a 235-acre camp and can choose from traditional camp activities as well as numerous outdoors specialties like survival techniques, outdoor living skills, rock climbing, and animal tracking. The camp is for boys and girls ages 9 through 12. Six one-week sessions run through the summer and cost $395 each. Those who register early receive a discount.

Older kids age 12 to 14 can choose a special camp called the Adventure Team. Campers spend the week backpacking, rappelling, orienteering, taking nature hikes, and learning to plan their own menus and pack their gear. The staff takes them on various trips, including one to hike and study nature in Lost Maples State Park and another to explore aquatics at Garner State Park. The camp also uses Robert's Ranch, a 1,000-acre spread in nearby Comfort. The ranch features various types of terrain, exotic wildlife, wildlife, and clear running streams ideal for fishing and small-ecosystem and nature study. This level of camping is intended to build team leadership and establish outdoor living and camping skills.

Camp Flaming Arrow offers advanced programs for older teens. Kids 15 and 16 enroll in the CIT (Counselor In Training) camp and work behind the scenes in the kitchen, office, and helping with younger kids. After this program, 16-year-olds advance to Leaders In Training and help coordinate activities and work more with the campers. Seventeen-year-olds are hired as paid Junior Counselors.

School groups can study year-round in the Highlife Program. The staff will work with individual schools or teachers to set up curricula in the outdoors such as team building, wildlife study, or adventure. They may use the camp's Environmental Education Center, set up for outdoor study and equipped with a kitchen, two baths, tables, and a mini-museum complete with pelts, hands-on displays, artifacts, bones, and plant and animal specimens.

Y.O. Adventure Camp [HC]
P.O. Box 555
Mountain Home, TX 78058
830-640-3220
Fax: 210-640-3348
Director—Dan Reynolds
C.A.M.P.

Located on 40,000 acres in the Hill Country, the Y.O. is a real rambling, working ranch. Not only does it have cattle, it has 60 to 65 different species of exotic animals, such as giraffes, zebras, and ostriches. Y.O. has two basic programs: a summer camp open to children age 7–16, and an environmental education camp for schools.

During summer camp, kids can participate in a wide variety of outdoor recreation activities, including a ropes course, a climbing tower, natural history study, hiking, farming/ranching, horseback riding, outdoor skills, archery, riflery, and canoe trips. Every camper also goes on a camp-out of their choice, where they cook their own meal and build their own fire. Y.O. takes up to sixty boys and girls age 7–16. There are two sessions available to kids, costing $1,100 for two weeks, or $650 for one week.

Those who opt for the two-week session spend the second

week concentrating on one of four topics. Campers can choose from Outdoor Skills such as shooting sports, Natural History Study, Adventure with skills like rock climbing, and Equestrian Camp. After the kids have practiced, the camp takes them on an outing to use their skills either on the premises or at another nearby location. For instance, a child who chooses rock climbing might get to culminate his or her studies with a trip to Enchanted Rock.

During the school year, school groups can book the camp for 1 to 9 days and choose from a list of activities to suit their needs. Some school groups may prefer scientific study, while others choose to emphasize adventure. In all camps, the staff also drives campers out to get a closer look at the exotic animals.